C000125471

September–December 2020

Edited by **Helen Paynter** and **David Spriggs**

The Bible Reading Fellowship
15 The Chambers, Vineyard
Abingdon OX14 3FE
brf.org.uk

The Bible Reading Fellowship (BRF) is a Registered Charity (233280)

ISBN 978 0 85746 736 2
All rights reserved

Distributed in Australia by:
MediaCom Education Inc, PO Box 610, Unley, SA 5061
Tel: 1 800 811 311 | admin@mediacom.org.au

Distributed in New Zealand by:
Scripture Union Wholesale, PO Box 760, Wellington
Tel: 04 385 0421 | suwholesale@clear.net.nz

Acknowledgements
Scripture quotations marked with the following acronyms are taken from the
version shown. Where no acronym is given, the quotation is taken from the version
stated in the contributor's introduction. NRSV: The New Revised Standard Version
of the Bible, Anglicised edition, copyright © 1989, 1995 by the Division of Christian
Education of the National Council of the Churches of Christ in the United States
of America. Used by permission. All rights reserved. NIV: The Holy Bible, New
International Version (Anglicised edition) copyright © 1979, 1984, 2011 by Biblica.
Used by permission of Hodder & Stoughton Publishers, a Hachette UK company.
All rights reserved. 'NIV' is a registered trademark of Biblica. UK trademark number
1448790. KJV: The Authorised Version of the Bible (The King James Bible), the
rights in which are vested in the Crown, are reproduced by permission of the
Crown's Patentee, Cambridge University Press. TNIV: The Holy Bible, Today's New
International Version, copyright © 2004 by Biblica. Used by permission of Hodder &
Stoughton Publishers, a division of Hodder Headline Ltd. All rights reserved. 'TNIV'
is a registered trademark of International Bible Society. ESV: The Holy Bible, English
Standard Version, published by HarperCollins Publishers, © 2001 Crossway Bibles,
a division of Good News Publishers. Used by permission. All rights reserved.

Every effort has been made to trace and contact copyright owners for material used
in this resource. We apologise for any inadvertent omissions or errors, and would
ask those concerned to contact us so that full acknowledgement can be made in
the future.

A catalogue record for this book is available from the British Library

Printed by Gutenberg Press, Tarxien, Malta

Suggestions for using *Guidelines*

Set aside a regular time and place, if possible, when and where you can read and pray undisturbed. Before you begin, take time to be still and, if you find it helpful, use the BRF Prayer on page 6.

In *Guidelines*, the introductory section provides context for the passages or themes to be studied, while the units of comment can be used daily, weekly or whatever best fits your timetable. You will need a Bible (more than one if you want to compare different translations) as Bible passages are not included. Please don't be tempted to skip the Bible reading because you know the passage well. We will have utterly failed if we don't bring our readers into engagement with the word of God. At the end of each week is a 'Guidelines' section, offering further thoughts about or practical application of what you have been studying.

Occasionally, you may read something in *Guidelines* that you find particularly challenging, even uncomfortable. This is inevitable in a series of notes which draws on a wide spectrum of contributors and doesn't believe in ducking difficult issues. Indeed, we believe that *Guidelines* readers much prefer thought-provoking material to a bland diet that only confirms what they already think.

If you do disagree with a contributor, you may find it helpful to go through these three steps. First, think about why you feel uncomfortable. Perhaps this is an idea that is new to you, or you are not happy about the way something has been expressed. Or there may be something more substantial – you may feel that the writer is guilty of sweeping generalisation, factual error, or theological or ethical misjudgement. Second, pray that God would use this disagreement to teach you more about his word and about yourself. Third, have a deeper read about the issue. There are further reading suggestions at the end of each writer's block of notes. And then, do feel free to write to the contributor or the editor of *Guidelines*. We welcome communication, by email, phone or letter, as it enables us to discover what has been useful, challenging or infuriating for our readers. We don't always promise to change things, but we will always listen and think about your ideas, complaints or suggestions. Thank you!

To send feedback, please email **enquiries@brf.org.uk**, phone **+44 (0)1865 319700** or write to the address shown opposite.

Writers in this issue

Rosie Button is a lecturer in member care and gender and mission at Redcliffe College in Gloucester. She has previously taught biblical studies and Greek in theological colleges in Zimbabwe and Uganda, as a Crosslinks mission partner.

Peter Phillips is research fellow in digital theology at Durham University and head of digital theology at Premier Media. His research focuses around the impact of digital culture on theology and on contemporary religious practice.

Derek Tidball is retired but continues to write, teach and preach. He pastored two Baptist churches and worked in theological education, here and overseas, culminating in twelve years as principal of London School of Theology.

Andy Angel is the vicar of St Andrew's, Burgess Hill. Previously, he taught New Testament in Church of England training colleges and has written various books, including *Intimate Jesus: The sexuality of God incarnate* (SPCK, 2017).

Helen Morris is a lecturer in applied theology at Moorlands College, where she is the course leader for BA programmes. Her PhD was in the area of contemporary ecclesiology. She has written *Flexible Church: Being the church in the contemporary world* (SCM Press, 2019).

Terry Griffith has been a Baptist minister for 40 years, pastoring two churches in London. He is also an associate research fellow at Spurgeon's College and has researched and published on the Johannine letters.

Kate Bruce is an RAF Chaplain. Her PhD is in preaching and imagination, and she regularly offers day conferences in preaching and leads retreats. She enjoys writing, running and performing stand-up comedy.

With a background in mission work in Asia, **David Kerrigan** is a Baptist minister, a governor of Spurgeon's College and, until 2017, was general director of the Baptist Missionary Society, now BMS World Mission.

After 20 years as a Baptist minister, **David Spriggs** held a number of posts at the Evangelical Alliance and Bible Society. On retiring, he has returned to local Baptist ministry in two churches in Leicestershire. For a number of years he was the editor of *Guidelines*.

Paul Williams is chief executive of Bible Society, having previously worked as an academic theologian. He is research professor of marketplace theology and leadership at Regent College, Canada, the visionary behind the ReFrame film series and the author of *Exiles on Mission* (Brazos, 2020).

Helen Paynter writes...

I am delighted to have several new writers to introduce to you this month. Terry Griffith has recently completed doctoral work on the Johannine letters. He brings us some of the fruit of his studies in two weeks of readings on these important, and often overlooked, letters. Rosie Button has written a thoughtful set of notes on leadership in the contemporary world, drawing on familiar and less-familiar themes from the life and letters of the apostle Paul.

We also have helpful contributions by two further new writers for us. In complementary readings, Paul Williams and Peter Phillips reflect on the relevance and interpretation of the Bible today. In an age when biblical literacy in the UK is at a deep low, these themes are important and relevant for us.

There are familiar names, too. Derek Tidball brings us a set of reflections on some of the richness of salvation – a theme ever to be explored, to be pondered and to draw us to worship. Derek's notes help us to do just that.

In Advent, another well-loved contributor, David Kerrigan, will be helping us to reflect on the meaning of the kingdom of peace: an ancient and glorious theme whose relevance seems more pressing with every passing year.

It is good to hear once again from the previous editor of *Guidelines*, David Spriggs. For Christmas week, David reflects on some of the readings from the traditional Festival of Nine Lessons and Carols, which for so many of us marks the beginning of our Christmas celebrations. David draws our attention to the original context of these well-known passages and helps us see how such an understanding deepens our appreciation of 'the loving purposes of God'.

While I've enjoyed and appreciated all the contributions, there are some which stand out for me. Andy Angel's work on Matthew is thought-provoking and illuminating. But it also had me (almost literally, if I weren't so British) standing up and yelling 'Amen!' He has conveyed something of the sharp call to discipleship that Jesus brought, which years of familiarity may have blunted.

I also loved Kate Bruce's thoughtful reflections on deep spirituality and how it might shape our mission. I appreciate not only the challenging perspectives that Kate offers, but also the really beautiful way that she writes.

Another contribution that had me standing up and applauding (silently) was Helen Morris' excellent set of readings highlighting some of the ways that contemporary biblical studies can enhance our understanding and appreciation of familiar biblical passages. As someone who believes firmly that 'the Lord has yet more light and truth to break forth from his word', it was wonderful to read Helen's eloquent demonstration of this.

I'm delighted to offer these notes to you. I hope you find them as helpful as I do. And I wonder which ones will have you standing up and yelling, 'Amen!' Do let us know.

The BRF Prayer

Almighty God,
you have taught us that your word is a lamp for our feet
and a light for our path. Help us, and all who prayerfully
read your word, to deepen our fellowship with you
and with each other through your love.
And in so doing may we come to know you more fully,
love you more truly, and follow more faithfully
in the steps of your son Jesus Christ, who lives and reigns
with you and the Holy Spirit, one God forevermore.
Amen

Were you there? BRF celebrates its centenary in 2022 and we'd love you to share your BRF memories with us. We've already heard from supporters with wonderful stories. Beryl Fudge attended our 25th anniversary service in Westminster Central Hall in 1947, in the presence of the Queen Mother and Princess Margaret. Catharine Heron was prepared for confirmation in 1945 by our founder, Canon Leslie Mannering, and still has his duplicated notes in their original brown cardboard folder.

Do you have a BRF story to tell, whether of events, people, books or Bible reading notes? Please email **eley.mcainsh@brf.org.uk**, call **01865 319708** or write to **Eley McAinsh** at BRF, 15 The Chambers, Vineyard, Abingdon OX14 3FE, United Kingdom.

Leaders in the contemporary world

Rosie Button

No one can deny that we live in interesting times. Whichever way you look in the public sphere, things seem to be in upheaval. Uncertainty about the future, disillusionment with the status quo and feelings of disenfranchisement abound. The world is changing at an alarming rate in other areas, for example as social media extends its reach and becomes an arena for heated disagreement, and as societal mores shift and change. Every sphere of life is affected by change, from the way we work and shop to the way we read the news and communicate with each other. The divide between those who have grown up in the digital age and those who predated it is stark, with much senior leadership still being in the hands of the older generations.

So church and mission inevitably have to change and adapt. The message does not change, for the truths of the gospel remain constant, and Jesus is the same, yesterday, today and forever, as we read in Hebrews 13:8. But how do we navigate the swirling waters of our postmodern world? How do we make sure we are engaging younger people and remaining relevant? And how do we reach out in mission to an increasingly post-Christian society? What kind of Christian leaders do we need for times like these?

In this set of notes, we look to Paul for inspiration. Studying some excerpts from his epistles, we will explore his example as a leader. Paul himself lived in times of change and threat. While we may see ourselves as living in almost post-Christian times, where long-held values and beliefs are no longer taken as read, Paul was leading the church's mission at the very outset of Christian history, when Christianity was brand new but equally countercultural – perhaps even more so than today. We can find in Paul's life guidance for mission and ministry that is remarkably relevant and encouraging.

Unless otherwise stated, Bible quotations are taken from the NRSV.

1 Passion for the gospel

Ephesians 3

In the first two chapters of Ephesians, Paul gives the glory to God for the rich blessings of the gospel, which he effusively describes. He extols how God out of his great love has made the Ephesians alive and united with him in Christ, bringing hope, peace and belonging, all purely by grace (2:11–22). The writing overflows with his exuberance and wonder at the gospel. In chapter 3 he asks them therefore not to be discouraged that he is writing to them from prison (v. 13). Anyone reading these verses can sense Paul's passion and utter confidence in the Lord. Indeed, in verse 12 he talks of the boldness with which we can pray to God and he then prays an incredible prayer for the Ephesians to be strengthened in their inner beings by the Spirit, have Christ in their heart, and know the breadth, length, height and depth of Christ's love (vv. 14–19).

I wonder how many of us as Christian leaders or teachers are this excited about the gospel? How many of us pray this fervently for the people we are ministering among? In the day-to-day of busy ministry it is rather easy to become a bit worn down by it all, overwhelmed by the task. When we reach the point of exhaustion, we can lose our love for the people we are serving and even our love for God.

There are some clues in Ephesians 3 as to how to retain the initial passion for our God-given task, even in challenging circumstances. Paul remembered that his task was a gift from God and that he was to do it by God's power and not his own. He remembered the big picture: God's plan spanned from creation, to reach through the church even the rulers in the heavenly places (how encouraging is that when things are looking bleak!). He approached God with ambitious prayers for his people, turning it all over to God and giving him the glory. He understood it was God's gift, God's power, God's plan, God's people, God's glory…

May we be renewed in our ministry by dwelling on these truths and by taking time to pray often, as Paul did, both for the people we are working with and for ourselves, asking God to rekindle in us the excitement and passion for the gospel that shines so clearly from Paul.

2 Authenticity and humility

2 Corinthians 11:24—12:10

The previous reading might have made it seem that Paul found it all easy. But another feature of Paul's leadership was his honesty about his inner struggles (e.g. Romans 7:15–20), and several times in letters he listed the hardships he faced. He was open about his successes and his failures.

This passage from 2 Corinthians is a good example of Paul keeping it real. On face value, it seems to be a strange mixture of boasting and humility. Paul is defending himself against an unfavourable comparison with the 'super-apostles' (11:5) by boasting as they do. But the accomplishments Paul 'boasts' of are hard work, imprisonments, floggings, threats to his life and weakness – although one recollection is different, where he speaks of the special revelation he once received. But even there he carefully reframes his words and says, 'On my own behalf I will not boast, except of my weaknesses' (12:5). In 12:7–9, he speaks of his famed 'thorn in the flesh', the unspecified recurring weakness that taught Paul the crucial lesson: 'My grace is sufficient for you, for power is made perfect in weakness.' We understand from this that it is when we admit our own limitations that God can truly work and his power be seen.

Today, especially among millennials, authenticity is seen as a key value. This means walking the talk, living out what we teach, but also being real about ourselves and our experiences. This is all the more important in a world where 'fake news' is a frighteningly familiar term, so that what we hear can't necessarily be believed, and where #MeToo revelations are uncovering hidden abuses from the past, so that people we thought we knew may not be trustworthy. Mark Meynell's book *Wilderness of Mirrors* shows how trust has been lost in leaders and authorities in our day, and this loss leads to a range of repercussions. Christian leaders must be different, offering an authentic witness to a trustworthy gospel. This means living godly lives in keeping with the moral teachings of the Bible, but also being honest about ourselves. The tendency towards celebrity culture in the Christian world is a problem in all of this. I am surely not alone in finding it most helpful when preachers talk about their own struggles. We need leaders who like Paul are humble enough to be honest about their successes and failures and own up to a total dependence on Christ.

3 Valuing partnerships in the gospel

Ephesians 4:1–16

My favourite bits of Paul's letters are near the end, where he often mentions his fellow workers. I love to try to picture them, although details are scant. Tychicus, Euodia and Syntyche, Clement and many more, notably including both men and women – Paul always worked alongside others, and our passage from Ephesians 4 reveals Paul's way of thinking about this.

In verses 1–6 Paul makes a plea for unity, highlighting with seven 'ones' that we Christians belong together as one body under one God and Father. But he goes on to say (vv. 7–12) that we have different gifts given to us by Christ – some are apostles, others prophets, evangelists, pastors and teachers – all for building up the body of Christ. Verse 16 details that every part has a role to play: 'The whole body, joined and knitted together… as each part is working properly, promotes the body's growth.' The 'body of Christ' passage in Romans 12 is similar, but the emphasis there is on valuing those who are different from you, while the emphasis here is on working and growing together, with everyone playing their part. Elsewhere, in 1 Corinthians 3, Paul urges the importance of working with rather than against others. Some regarded Apollos as Paul's rival. But, Paul says, 'I planted, Apollos watered, but God gave the growth… [We] have a common purpose… we are God's servants, working together' (1 Corinthians 3:6–9).

The idea of the 'heroic leader' ploughing ahead, drawing others in their wake, is nowadays being questioned. Eddie Gibbs' book *Leadership Next: Changing leaders in a changing culture* highlights the growing preference for teamwork and collaborative leadership. He says: 'Leadership is about connecting, not controlling… Discipling occurs not in isolation but in communities… the same is true of ministry; it flows from authentic community' (p. 93). In mission we have long been talking about partnering, realising both the pitfalls for the 'lone ranger missionary' and the utter necessity of cross-cultural workers coming alongside local churches and Christians, as Paul demonstrates so well in his own ministry and teaching. Perhaps at home as well, we should (as already happens in many places) look for ways to operate more as a team within our own churches, empowering a diversity of members to be more fully involved. Furthermore, can we collaborate with other churches and organisations in our areas, finding the creative synergy that comes from working with others who may be different from us?

4 Mentoring younger leaders

As well as the high value he places on his co-workers, another feature of Paul's leadership which is essential for today is his mentoring of emerging leaders. We see this most clearly in his letters to Timothy and Titus. Paul met Timothy in Lystra, identified him as a potential co-worker and invited him along on his ministry tour (Acts 16:1–4). From the many ensuing appearances of Timothy in Acts and the letters, we can see that Paul valued him as a member of his team (e.g. Acts 17:14; Philippians 2:19–20), giving him responsibilities and empowering him for ministry (1 Thessalonians 3:2).

In our passage from 1 Timothy, Paul has left Timothy, still a young man, in charge of the church in Ephesus and is writing to advise him in this role. He urges him to 'train yourself in godliness' and to ignore 'profane myths and old wives' tales', instead being 'nourished on the words of faith and of the sound teaching that you have followed' (vv. 6–7). He acknowledges that this involves 'toil and struggle' – as physical training also does (think 'no pain, no gain'). An equivalent word for young leaders today might be: work hard at studying the Bible and theology and at living them out, and be wary of the popular wisdom of our day.

In verse 12 Paul says, 'Let no one despise your youth, but set the believers an example.' Many a younger leader has doubtless experienced a flash of joy and affirmation reading these words. It is interesting that Paul entrusted the oversight of this church, not exactly a straightforward assignment, to the younger Timothy (probably in his early 30s). But he knew Timothy was well-trained and grounded in the scriptures, with a lot of experience as well as the qualities necessary for ministry – and while trusting him he continued to guide and advise him through his letters, as we have seen.

With the world changing rapidly, as mentioned in my introduction, it is clear that we need young people involved in Christian leadership. It is vital, and it is modelled in scripture, where we see God using men and women, young and old, in his mission. Mentoring is a way of learning leadership preferred by millennials, as the 2018 survey by Forge Leadership showed (**millennial-leader.com/research**). Paul's example of mentoring Timothy seems to be a highly relevant model for leadership development for us today.

5 Flexibility and creativity

1 Corinthians 8; 9:19–23

In my years working as a missionary in Central and East Africa, I often came back to this passage about 'food offered to idols' in 1 Corinthians 8. The underlying message, which helped me in cross-cultural situations there, is also helpful as we face cultural change in our own societies – that actually, as Christians, we have great freedom to be flexible. Paul made this even more explicit in his 'all things to all people' teaching in chapter 9. Regarding the food offered to idols, Paul concluded that we can either eat the food or not eat the food, depending on how it will affect the people we are with. Since 'no idol in the world really exists' (8:4), eating the offerings to them logically cannot do any harm. The thing to be avoided at all costs was if eating the food conveyed to others, who hadn't yet grasped this, that participating in idolatry was still a good thing to do, and so led them astray. Paul was guided in this by his love for the people and longing for their salvation.

It is the same love resulting in flexibility that enabled him to say in 9:19–23 that he became in different circumstances 'as a Jew', 'as one under the law' or 'one not under the law' and ultimately 'all things to all people' – so that he might by any means save some.

In today's complex and rapidly changing world, flexibility, adaptability and creativity are vital qualities for Christian leaders. While we rightly fear compromise, isn't it worth noting that it was love for the lost that drove the formerly dogmatic Paul to be open to change? Weighing up what are our freedoms and constraints as Christians is not easy, but we must be driven in this by love, courage and openness to the Holy Spirit, guided by careful study of scripture.

6 Resilience with joyfulness

Philippians 1:3–26

I was living in Zimbabwe at a time when the political situation became very tense, with rioting, shortages and runaway inflation. The phrase of the day was *zvakapresa!* – 'we are under pressure!' But people in general were so resilient, and one clergyman I remember always ended conversations with 'Hallelujah!' and by laughing – not cynically, but finding joy in God no matter what. Paul similarly shows a remarkable level of resilience and joy in his letter to the Philippians, written from a Roman prison.

In this passage he starts (vv. 3–11) by describing his prayers for the Philippian Christians, filled with thanks, joy and confidence. He prays that they will be filled with love, knowledge and insight, leading to a harvest of righteousness. Then from verse 12 onwards he explains how his imprisonment has actually led to a furtherance of the gospel, both through his own witness to the guards and others and through others who preach with their own agendas – but Paul rejoices in it, saying, 'What does it matter?… Christ is proclaimed in every way' (v. 18). Paul's unshakeable resilience and joyfulness in the light of his sufferings are captured in his well-known words in verse 21: 'For to me, living is Christ and dying is gain.'

There is no naive optimism on Paul's part, nor an attempt to grin and bear it, nor what an old friend used to call 'teddy-bear Christianity', pretending everything is happy. Paul was realistic about his possible death for the sake of the gospel. And he simply wasn't happy all the time – he mentions being anxious for people (e.g. 2:28) and sometimes tearful (3:18). But he had an underlying joy which shone through. The keys to it are found throughout chapter 1: thankfulness, confidence in the power of the gospel to save and transform, dependence on the Holy Spirit, love of Christ and certainty of an eternal destiny with him.

In our world today, there is much uncertainty about the future, confusion over current trends in society and even questions about the future of the church in an increasingly secular age. Christian leaders enter into these concerns with the same emotions as anyone. But we have the same gospel and the same Spirit that Paul had; if we can find the resilience and joy in them that he had, we can be a huge, much-needed encouragement to those around us in our day, as we testify to the source of our hope.

Guidelines

- Choosing only six of Paul's leadership traits to reflect on was a challenge! Perhaps you could carry out your own further study of Paul as a leader, as seen through his letters. You could also look at the narratives about Paul in Acts and see how the traits we have highlighted in these studies were borne out in his actions and ministry.

- With Paul, we easily miss the driving force behind his choices and actions, hidden in plain sight: his great love for God and for the people to whom he was sent, both those in his churches and those he had not yet reached, which made him willing to give up everything for them. Does that kind of love drive us in our ministries?

- Ministry and mission are challenging in our rapidly changing and increasingly secular times: we desperately need to engage with contemporary culture while holding out the unchanging truths of the gospel. Let us pray in earnest for our Christian leaders (and for ourselves) that we will be able to rise to this challenge, fuelled by love and guided by God's word and his Holy Spirit.

FURTHER READING

Ruth Haley Barton, *Strengthening the Soul of Your Leadership: Seeking God in the crucible of ministry* (IVP, 2008).

Eddie Gibbs, *Leadership Next: Changing leaders in a changing culture* (IVP, 2005).

Mark Meynell, *A Wilderness of Mirrors: Trusting again in a cynical world* (Zondervan, 2015).

Reading the Bible well today

Peter Phillips

In these notes, spread over two weeks, we are going to use Psalm 119 and a selection of passages from the New Testament to explore how we read the Bible within contemporary society. 2 Timothy 2:15 tells us that a good Christian (whom God has 'approved') is one 'who correctly handles the word of truth'. Indeed, in the next chapter, the author gives us the New Testament's clearest statement that engaging with the Bible is part and parcel of lifelong discipleship. But the psalmist emphasised that point hundreds of years earlier.

So the message is clear, if daunting! But how do we do this in a church where the Bible seems to be the preserve of the experts up front rather than the average person in the pew? How do we read the Bible in a world which dismisses scripture as outdated and passé, and when there seems to be little time available in our busy schedules?

In both the Hebrew Bible and New Testament times, people were more likely to hear the word than to read it, since much less than a quarter of the population could read. Over the years, religious communities often tried to teach reading through Bible engagement, but for many people the option was not there. For most of history, the Bible was mediated through drama, ritual, readings, arts and crafts, or discussions in village gatherings which developed into the synagogues of Jesus' day. This continued as the norm until reading became more widespread around the time of the Reformation. Today we have all the options in the world to engage with the Bible: through plentiful paper copies, through apps, online, through sound, through dramatisation, through art, at church, while commuting – basically anywhere at any time. But how do we read it well today?

Unless otherwise stated, Bible quotations are taken from the NIV.

1 Read the Bible with obedience

Psalm 119:1–24

Psalm 119 is the longest chapter in the Bible and the longest psalm. It was written as an acrostic poem, 22 units of eight verses, each starting with a different letter of the Hebrew alphabet. It is also a meditation on the scriptures, a rolling around of ideas through poetry, a rumination on the word of God.

Throughout the poem eight words are used to describe the scriptures: *torah* (law), *dabar* (word), *mispatim* (judgements), *edot* (testimonies), *misvot* (commandments), *huqqim* (statutes), *piqqudim* (precepts) and *imrah* (word). This may reflect the different aspects of the Bible – history, law, narrative, poetry, etc. – the different ways in which we engage with the Bible or how people in general engage with the Bible. Some see it as an instruction book, a list of rules or a handbook of life. Such views look for ways in which to live according to the Bible, to live biblical lives, and this is indeed how the psalm opens: 'Blessed are those… who walk according to the law of the Lord' (v. 1).

But the Bible is also a book of discipleship, guiding our walk with God. So the second section of the poem talks about young people staying 'on the path of purity… by living according to your word' (v. 9). The Bible doesn't just provide an entry point to discipleship; it also provides a way to stay on that route – the internalisation of the word, the statutes, the commands of God. The Bible doesn't just remain something which is outside of our lives; it is something that (as Jeremiah 31 reminds us) is written on our hearts.

Interestingly, the third stanza realises that without God discipleship is futile. That sounds strange, but look at what the psalmist says: 'Be good to your servant… that I may obey your word' (v. 17); 'I am a stranger… do not hide your commands from me' (v. 19). The psalmist calls out to God for help in keeping close to the scriptures. The word of God (both the written word but also the living Word) is the way to go. The word of God is the path of discipleship. But we also need the living Word of God to support us through his written word to keep on with our discipleship.

Where are you with God's word? Does the word hold you up? Do God's statutes guide you through your life as a disciple of Christ? Does the word work within you to lead you along the path of discipleship? Reflect on your own engagement with God's word in your life.

2 Read the Bible with delight

'I am laid low in the dust' (v. 25). The fourth section of this psalm starts on a low note. The psalmist talks of the sorrow in his own experience. In verse 28, he talks of his soul being weary with sorrow and in the next verse of their being some danger that he will fall into deceitful ways. But we are not told why. He is not, here, surrounded by people who are pulling him down. He doesn't blame fools or Satan. He just points out that this is part of his life, part of his daily experience. He is low in mood; perhaps he is even experiencing some form of depression.

Note that his answer is to reach out to God – 'preserve my life according to your word' (v. 25); 'teach me your decrees' (v. 26); 'strengthen me according to your word' (v. 28). He is feeling low and calls out to God in his distress. But the reason he can call out to God is because he is aware of what God's word says about God. He can be certain of how God acts. He knows that when Miriam and Rachel, Moses and David cried out to God, he helped them. So, 'according to your word', the psalmist too knows that God will save.

In verse 35, we see a change come over the psalmist's words: 'Direct me… for there I find delight.' What does it mean to know delight in God's word? Or, more mysterious still, what does it mean to know even in a low mood the delight of God, the delight in his word, the assurance that all will be well because God is faithful?

3 Read the Bible with thanks

Psalm 119:41–64

Another day, another set of readings and another pronouncement of God's unfailing love. The psalmist is so rooted in the word of God that he knows God's love, his salvation, never fails. He knows God's love is unfailing, so he can ignore the taunts of those around him. He isn't looking for affirmation from them, because all his affirmation comes from God his Saviour.

His anchor in the word – his delight for God's commands – gives him freedom to walk about, to speak to kings, to have no shame. And when mockers mock, his faith in the scriptures remains solid and unshakeable. God's word has become a song wherever the psalmist lodges. His obedience is the way he lives his life.

Reading the Bible should be something we do with joy in our hearts and with gratitude. God has spoken to us. Corrie ten Boom, a protector of Jews in the Netherlands during the war, who herself miraculously survived Ravensbrück concentration camp, once said that the Bible is God's love letter to us. We have seen how God gives his word for our comfort, our sustenance and our encouragement. But so often, as Paul found with the Corinthians, we can decide that we are wise enough and do not need the guidance – we know best! Psalm 119 steers well clear of that kind of attitude. The psalmist remains constantly aware of his need of God and is thankful that God will not let him down.

Are you grateful for God's word? Why? What has helped you to come to that attitude? Is this something you could share with others, with your church, with your family and friends? Can you share your gratefulness in order to encourage others to be more grateful?

4 Read the Bible with openness

Engaging with the Bible is meant to make a difference to your life. Things change when God's word is involved. We shouldn't be surprised at this, since his word created everything. It is creative: it brings order out of chaos, light from darkness, joy from sorry, life from death. It's too easy to split up God's word, when in fact each form – written, spoken, incarnate – are all communications of God's majestic presence. In other words, God's word is God's presence among us; it is his voice speaking into our lives and making a difference to us.

Again and again in this psalm we see the moral and social improvement which engaging with the word brings into the psalmist's life. But it also brings goodness into the psalmist's wider community. God's word seeds justice and goodness wherever it is shared. Like the sower sowing his seed, broadcasting it across the field and the path to maximise his yield, so too we are called to share the word of God with the world.

But the only way to share his word is to receive that word in the first place, to be open to the word, to embrace the word. Look at how the psalmist in verses 81–84 longs to receive God's blessing all over again. He is thirsty, he faints, his eyes fail. He is completely open to receiving all that God wants to share with him.

Such a longing is rare in our contemporary society, where we are used to having our full of whatever we want. We want for nothing; we wait for nothing. But that means that we can shut ourselves off from God as well – we can feel we've had enough and only want to engage on our terms rather than on God's terms. We thank God for all his blessings, which are now enough. We will come back to God when we need him. This is a mockery of true openness to God. True openness is an awareness of God's bounty, an awareness of God's presence, an awareness of God's grace.

Open your eyes, see Jesus. Open your ears, hear the word. Open your hearts, receive the Lord.

5 Read the Bible with praise

Psalm 119:89–112

The opening of this reading almost reflects the beginning of John's gospel – 'In the beginning was the Word, and the Word was with God, and the Word was God' (John 1:1). In the psalm we are told, 'Your Word, Lord, is eternal; it stands firm in the heavens' (v. 89). Both verses are connecting God's word with his eternal nature. God's speech, God's message of love and God's faithfulness are part and parcel of God's eternal character. But this means that the scriptures, too, share in the character and eternity of God and therefore the praise that is due to him.

I remember the days when in some churches the Bible was brought in at the beginning of the service and everyone stood: a sign of respect. Or does it go further than respect and turn into honour, even praise? But it seems wrong to praise a book – despite the calls in the Reformation for our theology to be solely through scripture ('*sola scriptura*'). Some critics of Protestantism warn against bibliolatry, the literal worship of the Bible, since worship is reserved for God alone. But does that undermine the fact that the scriptures, as God's word, also bear something of his character? Is it going too far to say that we should also read the Bible with praise?

We read the Bible and praise God, even if we do not praise the Bible itself. But note how much of the language urges us to go further than saying that the Bible is just another book. The scriptures are 'a lamp for my feet, a light on my path' (v. 105). The scriptures guide the reader closer to God. And for this, God, the author of the text, deserves our praise and honour.

6 Read the Bible with hope

Psalm 119:129–152

Reading the Bible is about more than information gathering; reading the Bible is connecting with God. That in itself is a huge concept. Imagine having access to the living God. That's one of the greatest privileges of the Christian faith: we have access to God. Remember Revelation 3 and the letter to the Laodiceans. The writer rebukes the Laodiceans for being lukewarm about their faith, but then declares that Jesus stands at the door and knocks; that he shares a meal with whoever opens the door. Indeed, the letter moves on to offer the victorious the right to sit on a throne in heaven. The very next chapter opens with talk of a door open in heaven, beyond which lies the worshipping community.

In other words, the correct response to Jesus leads to worship. The acknowledgement of the one who is truly on the throne leads to worship. The churches in Asia Minor, in danger of preferring to see Caesar on the throne than God, are told that listening to God's summons opens us the benefits of the kingdom.

The psalmist calls out at night for God to help; he puts hope in God's word and declares that God is near. Although we may never see God, we know him through his word. He is near to us in his word. All we need to do is to pick up the book and read and let ourselves hear the word of God speaking encouragement to us – the hope of God with us.

Guidelines

Psalm 119 is a messy but beautiful psalm. Some of the messiness is because the author is trying to solve his own puzzle of saying something which begins with the right letter. But the messiness also looks a bit like waves rolling on to the shore, with similar themes coming back again and again and again: gratitude to God for communicating with us through his word; delight in God's provision of his word to resource our discipleship; the protecting nature of the word, which gives us the courage to withstand opposition and persecution; love for the word, which fills us with its very presence.

The devotion to God's word by the psalmist is telling. He sounds as though he is in love with the word, as though he is in relationship with the word. When CODEC, the research centre at Durham University which I helped establish, did a survey of millennial attitudes to the Bible, we asked them what relationship they had with the Bible. Many of them failed to answer the question. They didn't see the Bible as something you have a relationship with. It seemed to be source material for wisdom or a rule book for life. You don't need to have a relationship with your microwave's instruction booklet. But perhaps that is the issue here: that we have missed the point.

We need to hear deep in our hearts what Corrie ten Boom said about the scriptures: they are love letters from God. Perhaps some of our hesitation in reading the Bible well is because we are reading it like an instruction booklet rather than as love letters. In the next week, we'll continue our exploration by looking at some New Testament passages which guide our engagement with the scriptures.

1 Read the Bible regularly

James 1:16–27

The Centre for Bible Engagement in the USA conducted a series of surveys designed to explore how reading the Bible regularly affected the behaviour of those doing the reading. The stats are persuasive: 57% were less likely to get drunk, 68% less likely to have extramarital sex, 61% less likely to watch porn and 78% less likely to gamble. We see this in the letter to James as well – the importance of having the word of God planted within us: 'Humbly accept the word planted in you, which can save you' (v. 21).

To be fair, we cannot be certain what James means by this phrase. To have the word planted in us could mean having the presence of Jesus living in our hearts. Or it could mean having the word of God written on our hearts as part of the new covenant about which Jeremiah prophesied (Jeremiah 31). Or it could mean regularly and persistently studying the word of God. Whatever it is, it has the power to save us.

Bible reading, sadly, is in decline. But what might happen if we engage with the word – if we 'stoop over' ('look intently into', v. 25) the word, as James suggests, and continue to do this – to engage with the word regularly in depth? The teachers mentioned in the Bible were teaching people how to read the texts. We know that by Augustine's time, the church seemed to have some form of literacy scheme in place to help the congregations learn more about the Bible and read it too.

Reading the Bible regularly allows the Bible to seep into our souls. It becomes part of our thinking, part of our reasoning, part of our morality. We get better and better at doing biblical reasoning to help us make biblical decisions about our lifestyle and our practice. And, as James says, for those who read the Bible intensely and continue to do so, 'they will be blessed in what they do'.

Reading the Bible regularly makes you less likely to sin, more likely to hear God and more likely to be blessed by him.

2 Read the Bible socially

We have quite a bit of evidence about the practices of the early church, both from Acts and from extrabiblical sources like Pliny and the Didache, a book of teaching written sometime around the turn of the first century. This evidence again and again points to the gathering together of the church. The word 'synagogue' means a social gathering, a coming together, and so the church kept up this pattern of faith.

Acts 2:42 talks of the disciples being devoted to the apostles' teaching and gathering together for fellowship. So too this passage describes the Jews of Berea reading the scriptures every day to see whether Paul was telling the truth. Pliny, the Roman governor of what is now northern Turkey, talks of the Christians gathering together before sunset to sing hymns, much like the pattern offered by Paul in 1 Corinthians 14. The Didache (which refers to the teaching of the apostles) notes that Christians meet together on the first day of the week to break bread together.

Although this seems to be the norm, there was clearly some pressure to drift away from the church, and the author of the letter to the Hebrews has to remind them not to stop meeting together, as some are (Hebrews 10:25). The drift away from the church that is warned about in Hebrews is a very clear reality in our time, as people drift away from what they regard as a boring church, irrelevant to the current needs of our society.

But meeting together is crucial; take a coal out of the fire and it will stop burning. This is not to diminish the experience of those who are housebound, ill or not independently mobile, though they might need to meet together more online than offline. They may create fellowship groups to meet together or make use of virtual spaces such as Facebook or Second Life. Some fresh expressions of church, along with communities focused on highly networked individuals, might also feel that it is culturally appropriate to meet more online – perhaps communicating through social media.

However we do it, meeting is most important – sharing in fellowship with other Christians around the Bible. This should be the staple diet for the church.

3 Read the Bible wisely

What does the author mean when he talks of one 'who correctly handles the word of truth' (2:15) – or the KJV translation, 'rightly dividing the word of truth'? The original Greek is a craftsman's term – to cut something straight, to divide two pieces down the middle, and so to handle things well. We are called to take the Bible carefully, wisely. My colleague in Durham, Richard Briggs, has written a whole book with this title, in which he focuses on different ways we might approach the biblical text. Of course, the Bible is many things to many people and contains a plethora of different types of text. But that's the point – let history be history, let biography be biography, let wisdom be wisdom. You need to recognise the kind of text you are dealing with before you seek to engage with it – you should not read Acts the same way you read Revelation.

'Handling the word correctly' is also about correctly discerning how we apply what we know of the scriptures in our daily lives. But to handle it correctly means that you need to know the text in the first place. Timothy, says the author, has known about the scriptures all of his life, from his infancy (3:15), taught to him by his grandmother Lois and his mother Eunice (1:5). Timothy has had a whole lifetime absorbing the scriptures and so now is in the right place to 'rightly divide the word'. Note that it is not that he has a degree in theology or that he has done 27 online courses on the Bible. What matters is that he has filled himself with the Bible – like the psalmist who wrote Psalm 119. He spends so much of his time reading and meditating on the verse that he has become part and parcel of it. Blessed are they who have spent their lives immersed in the scriptures.

In Ray Bradbury's novel *Fahrenheit 451*, a repressive regime decides to burn all books (451 degrees is the temperature at which paper burns). In order to salvage some of the best literature, a number of people take up the task of remembering the text word for word. Each person *becomes* the book. There are lots of churches which still recommend the memorising of scripture. But whether or not that is something we do, we would be wise to read the Bible more often, more closely, more wisely.

4 Read the Bible seriously

Hebrews 11:1–16

As we all know, taking something seriously means commitment and time. Learning a new skill, we are led to believe, takes 10,000 hours. But I think it also takes some innate ability and a determination to achieve the goal you set out to achieve. Hebrews 11 talks about faith as if it were part and parcel of the life of all the characters there, from Abel through to David. Notice that they act through faith – faith is a quality they possess.

The other day I did an icebreaker before the church service, and one of the tasks was to find someone in the church who had the gift of faith. I think out of a congregation of 50 regular church attenders, only a couple were willing to own up to having the gift of faith. I wondered why. 1 Corinthians 12:9 includes faith among the gifts of the Spirit, Ephesians 2:8 reminds us that faith is a gift of God and Hebrews 11 lists those exemplars of faith. If we are believers, we have the gift of faith. As we saw, the faithful in Hebrews 11 act out of an awareness of faith in their lives.

So why didn't the congregation feel the same? A lack of awareness of what the Bible says about faith? A lack of confidence in their own faithfulness?

But the gift of faith, as we see in Corinthians and Ephesians and, in practice, in Hebrews, is something different from worrying about whether we are holy enough. The gift of faith is God's gift to us, not because we earn it but because we live it. God gives us faith so that we can be holy. Our confidence needs to rest in the promises of God. Our faith needs to reflect its givenness. And that depends upon taking the Bible seriously.

This might mean taking the Bible a little bit more literally than is sometimes the case in the wider church. In our thinking over the last few days, we've talked about the Bible as God's words to us, as God addressing us. We will always want to take the Bible seriously because of that. How could we not? The living God reaches out to talk to us. Søren Kierkegaard, a Danish theologian from the 19th century, spoke of his delight that in the Bible the living God addressed him, even him! That is both a huge privilege, that God addresses us, but also a huge responsibility. For if God is speaking to us through the Bible, we need to ensure that we listen carefully and take what God is saying to heart. God himself is writing us love letters. We need to read the Bible seriously, because only that means that we are taking God seriously as well.

5 Read the Bible artfully

How does a passionate passage from Galatians 3 end up being entitled 'Read the Bible artfully'? When Paul says that before their very eyes 'Christ was clearly portrayed' (v. 1), the allusion is to painting – when Paul preaches he paints the scene, he takes you to the cross. Imagine that. In the early church, there were few visual images at hand. Most churches remained small and local, and so a converted villa was more likely to host the church than anything like a modern church building. The pictures to help the teaching needed to come from the preacher rather than the latest clip art. As such, Paul's own preaching and thus his teaching in the letters seem to be focused on giving people good mental images – e.g. the body, the remnant – rather than relying on people to just understand the words themselves. Thus he resorts to badgering and even insulting the Galatians and claiming they have been bewitched – more picturesque language.

There are plenty of such places in the Bible which show how the arts and Bible study go together. It may be that you could develop some artistic ways of engaging with the Bible. Research into active learning, doing something while you learn, shows how much doodling, creativity and beauty help us to engage with the subject we are trying to learn. Hence the importance of doodling Bibles or Bibles with large margins in which we can make notes or simply express ourselves in other ways.

You could paint your Bible reading, write a poem about it or send a letter to a friend. Getting creative allows your mind to focus on another part of the text, another dimension of the study. And there are lots of examples of how to do things well – although do you need to do it well or just well enough? Some of the best art I have ever seen spent years stuck on the fridge door after the kids brought it home from school or church.

6 Read the Bible with Jesus

Luke 24:13–35

It's worth thinking about how Jesus engaged with people about the Bible. The gospels are full of fulfilment stories, confirmation stories where Jesus actually goes beyond what the law has said and stories taken from the Old Testament and applied to the new situation Jesus is in. This story from Luke's gospel is especially important for its reminder that we need to spend time with Jesus and allow him to recount the gospel to us. Or perhaps that we need to make sure that we infuse our quiet time not just with reading the Bible, but also with reading the Bible with Jesus at our side.

The two disciples start out doing all the talking, and Jesus leads them into their account of what has happened in Jerusalem. He, rather surprisingly, rebukes them both for their lack of faith and their apparent ignorance before launching into an evidently detailed account ('beginning with Moses and all the Prophets') of what the scriptures say about him. The disciples are amazed and invite him to stay for a meal. He does and when he breaks bread, they suddenly realise who he is.

Two things to note. First, it is always good to have Jesus by your side to show you the depth and breadth of the Bible's meaning. I think that means being open to the Spirit when we are studying his word. Ask Jesus to make the Bible clearer to you, to make your own thinking deeper, to make you more like him. But also spend time in worship when you are studying the Bible, have something of the sacrament with you (bread and wine) and remind yourself that you are in worship mode. I know many ministers who create prayer spaces in their homes to help them engage more deeply both with God and with his word, the Bible.

Guidelines

Dietrich Bonhoeffer argues [that] the presence of Christ is the presence of the Word at the heart of the church. This enables preaching; this enables the sacraments; this enables everything. The Word of God is not just the testimony about Jesus but is in fact the very presence of Jesus and his presence makes real the Word of God. Jesus Christ is everything. As such, for Bonhoeffer discipleship is simply following Christ. There is no other content: no programme, no new law. He focuses on the call of Matthew and notes that Matthew's decision to leave the tax booth without any consideration of the implications was an unreasonable decision. It was not just a change of faith, as such, but also a practical change of direction in the way that he lived his life (Matthew 9:9–13). Just so, argues Bonhoeffer: the first step to discipleship is complete obedience – obedience to the call of Jesus; obedience to Jesus' commands to love; obedience to Jesus in everything. Discipleship for Bonhoeffer is a reliving of the life of the original disciples, and his writing on discipleship is dominated by his exegesis of the gospels.

Peter Phillips, *Engaging the Word*, p. 114

In these readings, we have built upon our reflections on Psalm 119 with various verses from the New Testament. We've looked at different ways to look at the Bible – in terms of both our approach and our methodology. We've seen that the Bible is best read regularly and socially, wisely and seriously, artfully and with Jesus. Overall, we have focused a good deal on the nature of the Bible as God's communication to us – like Bonhoeffer arguing that the real presence of Jesus is known to us in the presence of the written word. Moreover, like Bonhoeffer, we note that the path of discipleship begins with reading the word and continues with reading the word – much like the disciples on the road to Emmaus found.

It might be a good thing to reflect on your own approach to the Bible. Reflect on the presence of Jesus next time you come to read the text and draw close to him as he draws close to you.

FURTHER READING

Richard Briggs, *Reading the Bible Wisely* (Cascade Books, 2011).

Ellen Davis, *Getting Involved with God: Rediscovering the Old Testament* (Cowley Books, 2001).

Gordon Fee and Douglas Stuart, *How to Read the Bible for all Its Worth* (Zondervan, 2014).

Paula Gooder, *Searching for Meaning: An introduction to interpreting the New Testament* (SCM Press, 2008).

Peter Phillips, *Engaging the Word: Biblical literacy and Christian discipleship* (BRF, 2018).

Salvation 20:20

Derek Tidball

The long plot line of the Bible is all about salvation. The story begins with the creator God bringing all life into being and forming human beings as the climax of his work. The plan was that people should have an open and trusting relationship with him. Alas, all went wrong from the earliest time, causing a disruption between God and his creatures, and their alienation from each other and the world over which they presided. The consequences were dire, not only for the people involved and subsequent generations but also for creation itself. As a result, God plans and executes a rescue mission, which becomes the deep plot line of scripture.

The rescue mission takes many forms, culminating in the coming of Jesus, who sacrificed himself to provide the ultimate answer. Previous solutions hadn't failed so much as provided preliminary sketches of the masterpiece to be unveiled in Christ. His work made possible the reconciliation of human beings with their creator and the restoration of the fallen creation under God's beneficial rule.

'Salvation' is the short-hand term for this rescue mission, which can be viewed from many angles and which we can never fully exhaust. Salvation contains 'the boundless riches of Christ' (Ephesians 3:8). Here we only skim the surface. We don't, for example, give attention to the phases of salvation. Salvation is a past event; Paul asserts that 'he saved us' (Titus 3:5). Yet it's also an ongoing experience, not yet complete; hence, Paul talks of those 'who are being saved' (1 Corinthians 1:18). It's equally a future experience; to the Philippians, Paul says, 'Our citizenship is in heaven. And we eagerly await a Saviour from there' (Philippians 3:20).

We can't say it all, but at least we can begin to explore this great theme of salvation.

Unless otherwise stated, Bible quotations are taken from the NIV.

1 Salvation envisaged

Genesis 3:1–19

The Hebrew mind, as reflected in the Genesis narrative, shows little interest in philosophic speculation about the origin of evil. It simply asserts that God's perfect creation is spoiled by an alien presence, a serpent, who tempts Eve and consequently Adam to mistrust God and declare independence from him. The result is that they set in train a sequence of curses which impact their relationship with God, with each other and with the physical creation for ill.

Extraordinarily, however, the spelling out of the judgement which inevitably follows their disobedience contains the seed of hope. While not altogether sharp in focus, verse 15 suggests that no sooner has the problem of sin occurred than a solution is in sight. The verse contains several puzzles and is understood in different ways. Some see it as no more than a primitive explanation as to why human beings hate snakes and, apparently, vice versa. But that seems unlikely, given the setting of the saying. Others see it as pointing to the coming of a Messiah who will rescue people from the enemy, who initiates and continues to stimulate evil. This is even clearer if 'offspring' is singular (pointing to one person) rather than plural (pointing to more than one). Is 'crush' the right interpretation on both occasions in the two lines of the verse, or is that claiming too much, since the word may only mean 'strike at' or 'batter'?

What's clear is that the curse condemns humanity to ongoing hostility between humans and the serpent, who is described more fully later as Satan, the tempter and accuser, who leads people astray (Revelation 12:9; 20:2). Early Christians echoed this verse, believing that God 'will soon crush Satan under your feet' (Romans 16:20). They saw Christ as the last Adam (1 Corinthians 15:45), an individual yet corporate figure, removing the question as to whether 'offspring' is singular or plural. If initially they weren't courageous enough to claim the offspring would utterly crush the serpent, they at least believed he would put up a good fight. The New Testament fills out the picture, confidently asserting that Christ has utterly defeated Satan (Colossians 2:15; Hebrews 2:14–15). Not without reason has this verse been called 'the first gospel' (*protoevangelium*).

2 Salvation as election

The world got further and further away from God's plan for it, with violence and corruption multiplying (Genesis 6:5). How was God going to rescue the situation? God acted to create a fifth column of new humanity who would follow his commands. While he entered a preliminary covenant with Noah, his main plan was routed through the family of Abram (later called Abraham).

The choice of Abraham prefigures the later, fuller understanding of salvation as God's election. There was nothing special, as far as we know, about Abraham which made him and his family worthy of being chosen. They were average pagans, devoted to the worship of the usual Chaldean deities, when the living God called them to leave their hometown of Ur and travel to Canaan to commence a new race of people who would experience a special relationship with him, involving mutual obligations.

Three things stand out about this new phase of God's relation to his world. First, the covenant required a positive response from Abraham which involved leaving one life, travelling to a new location and living in a different way. Second, the covenant was the channel through which God was going to 'bless' Abraham and his family, that is, prosper them in every way and make them a significant and populous nation. Third, the purpose of the covenant was that they could channel God's well-being to others, in fact, to 'all peoples on earth' (12:3). The intention was never that they would receive God's blessing for selfish ends or to mark their superior status, but always that they should serve the wider world.

Their election gave them a significant role at the time and for generations to come, but also became a model for the salvation we enjoy today in Christ. The idea of Christians being 'called' is widespread in apostolic teaching, while Romans 8:29–30 and Ephesians 1:3–10 develop the idea, applying it to our salvation. As with Abraham, our calling requires us to response to God's unexpected and undeserved initiative and to undergo radical transformation, living in obedience to his commands. This new covenant is the means by which God will dispense his bounty on the whole of our lives for good. And its purpose is not that we may selfishly enjoy our own salvation, but that we may be the conduit of God's blessing to others.

3 Salvation as deliverance

From early days, God warned Abraham that his promise of blessing would not be fulfilled in a straightforward manner, but that his descendants would experience 400 years of slavery in 'a country not their own' before they entered the promised land (Genesis 15:13). When that time had passed, the children of Israel were liberated from bondage in Egypt and began their journey to take possession of Canaan. Their departure from Egypt's grip was the dramatic climax of a series of contests between Pharaoh and Moses, God's appointed deliverer, and the spiritual powers they represented. Ever since, the children of Israel, and their spiritual heirs, Christian believers, have looked back on the exodus as the paradigm for understanding salvation.

Several key elements are captured in the Passover supper and their midnight escape. Its focus is on salvation as deliverance from oppression, liberation from hostile forces. That deliverance will take many forms – individual, corporate and cosmic – as the story unfolds further. It stresses that liberation takes place as a result of God's powerful action, not as a result of political events or human effort. The surrounding chapters stress that it is God who 'brings out', 'redeems', 'rescues', 'delivers' and 'saves' his people.

This story powerfully portrays the way in which there can be no salvation without cost. For the liberated Israelites, the cost is paid by the perfect Passover lamb they sacrifice and eat. For the Egyptians, there's equally a cost in their stubborn refusal to cooperate with God's desire for people to live in freedom rather than under oppression. Tragically the cost is that of their own firstborn. Salvation involves the shedding of blood. Furthermore, it demonstrates that there can be no salvation for the oppressed without judgement being meted out on their oppressors. Egypt's treatment at God's hand is no more than the treatment they had exacted from Israel. Punishment and salvation, to use James Denney's image, is 'as inseparable as heat from fire or the inside and outside of a cup' (*The Epistles to the Thessalonians*, Hodder & Stoughton, 1899, p. 292).

The exodus is the prototype of the greater liberation of people from all oppression through the sacrifice of Christ, *the* Passover lamb, as he bore the judgement for a sinful humanity where oppression is offensive to God but all too common among humans.

4 Salvation as cleansing

Leviticus 16

Once the Israelite tribes were liberated, they organised themselves into an embryonic nation, centred around a mobile tent which served as the seat of the living God. A complex cycle of sacrifices and ceremonies taught them spiritual truth by way of analogy, majoring on the question of atonement, that is, how to repair any disruption of relationship between the people and their God. One ceremony stood out as the unique high point of Israel's liturgical calendar, the annual Day of Atonement.

It was an elaborate ritual in which every detail counted. At its heart lay the entry of the high priest into the innermost room in the sanctuary, usually called the Most Holy Place. There, protected by clouds of incense, he sprinkled the blood of a sacrificed goat seven times on the cover of the ark of the covenant, the very throne of God himself. Afterwards, hands were laid on a second goat, chosen by lot, which was then led outside the camp, removing all the sins of the Israel from its midst and taking them back to the wilderness, the place of uncleanness.

While known sin and uncleanness was atoned for throughout the year, in various rituals, this annual spiritual 'spring clean' atoned for *all* the sins of Israel, including those which, for whatever reason, may have been overlooked. This is emphasised in verses 20–22. Among other elements of truth, it is teaching that sin contaminates God's dwelling place, as well as his people, and drives God from his throne. The rituals of this day brought about a deep cleansing which enable God to resume his rightful place at the centre of their community. Without it, Israel would be lost and the deliverance from Egypt would have been futile. They needed to experience salvation again, viewed here as cleansing from moral and spiritual defilement.

Two things about God become very evident. He is an awesome and holy God, to be approached with care, as the instructions to the high priest made clear. But he is also generous in his mercy. He provides people, unable to help themselves, with a simple way forward, though a blood sacrifice (as with the Passover) and a substitute scapegoat. So 'all their sins' (v. 21) were removed, leaving no room for doubt or uncertainty in their renewed relationship.

5 Salvation as pardon

Isaiah 52:13—53:12

From Isaiah's viewpoint, the healing of Israel's suffering would take place through the work of God's 'servant'. While scholars used to identify four passages in Isaiah as 'servant songs' (42:1–4; 49:1–6; 50:4–9; 52:13—53:12), they now recognise that the word 'servant' is not restricted to them. Nonetheless, the fourth song stands out as a classic celebration of the work of salvation brought about by the servant.

Addressed to the children of Israel facing the crisis of exile in Babylon, with all the questions it threw up about God's election of them and his faithfulness, the song acknowledges the very real suffering they were enduring (52:4). It explains, however, that they were the cause of their own suffering, for they had chosen to stray from God and live in their own way, rather than his (53:6). Such wilful independence from their covenant God unleashed inescapable consequences, which Isaiah views through the lens of rebellion and punishment. Where was salvation to be found?

Salvation was to come through the 'servant', who would quite unjustly, and cruelly, bear the weight of their sins and unprotestingly serve as their substitute in carrying the penalty for other's wrongdoing. The servant would play the role of the old atonement offerings outlined in the law of Israel. To all appearances, his life would be under God's curse, even though he had done nothing to merit it himself. The result of his self-sacrifice was that sick people would be cured, burdened people would be relieved, warring people would be offered peace and culpable people would be pardoned (53:5). His suffering would be redemptive.

Isaiah nowhere identifies who this servant is. Several suggestions have been made, including Jeremiah and Isaiah himself. Many believed it spoke of Israel itself, whose suffering in exile (and subsequently) was seen as redemptive. But the early Christians had no hesitation in saying that it was a prophecy about Jesus who, alone, fits the details of the song completely. In Luke 22:37 Jesus applied it to himself. Matthew saw Jesus in it (Matthew 8:17), and there are several other allusions connecting it to Jesus in the New Testament. Supremely, when the Ethiopian official asked Philip who Isaiah was referring to, Philip immediately 'told him the good news about Jesus' (Acts 8:35). His suffering brings about our forgiveness and pardons our sins.

6 Salvation as reversal

Isaiah's later chapters speak in magnificent and varied ways of the day when Israel's sentence of exile in Babylon would be brought to an end and she would be restored to her homeland. They speak of it in terms of being a second exodus – an act of God's deliverance as momentous as the earlier escape from Egypt. Isaiah 61 views it as Israel enjoying a total reversal of their fortunes. The good news of salvation – the word is used in 52:7 – would finally silence the stern voice of God's disfavour.

Salvation was to be the work of the Messiah, the one anointed by God's Spirit and empowered to bring it about peacefully through political changes on the international stage. Isaiah celebrates the impact it would have on individuals (vv. 1–3), seeing it as the arrival of 'the year of the Lord's favour' (v. 2), which is a reference to the Jubilee year spelled out in Leviticus 25, when debts were remitted. He celebrates the restoration of Israel's collective life, both in their cities and rural communities (vv. 4–6). Instead of being an international pariah, nations would hasten to their doors and enrich them. Confident joy in their inheritance would displace the shame and disgrace they had borne (v. 7). God would initiate this reversal because his character was one of commitment to justice, faithfulness and righteousness (vv. 8–9, 11). The prophet's response, understandably, is to rejoice in God's salvation and to revel in it, just as one does at a wedding (v. 10).

Jesus applied these words to himself in his home synagogue, thereby making the claim to be the Messiah (Luke 4:14–21). They become the programmatic statement of Luke's gospel, which repeatedly speaks of salvation as a reversal of people's struggles and demonstrates Jesus actually bringing it about. Salvation is Luke's major theme from the start, when Mary identifies God as 'my Saviour' (1:47) and Jesus' birth is announced as the birth of 'a Saviour' (2:11). Salvation is good news for the poor, humble, powerless, downtrodden, marginalised and unclean who, because of the Messiah, will exchange places with the rich, proud, powerful and self-righteous who think they have a special place in God's affection. Salvation means the first, as judged by normal human standards, will be last and the last, first.

Guidelines

The story of Israel has begun to show how rich and multifaceted our understanding of salvation can be. Yet the variety of insights form a coherent picture with a sharp focus. Salvation is about deliverance from human brokenness, which expresses itself in a variety of human experiences. Salvation occurs because God steps in and acts to set people free. That freedom leads to a restoration of relationship with him.

Numerous implications follow. One is the need to understand the cause and range of human brokenness. The biblical word for this is sin, but sin manifests itself in different ways, from being outrightly rebellious against God, living wickedly, being ignorant of him, being less than God intended us humans to be, being corrupted, through to simply being lost in his world. In the light of this, we might discuss how we would define the nature of sin today. What concepts of sin make most sense in 'guilt-free' societies? How best can we explain to those who do not accept God's right to determine how we should live that sin matters and is detrimental to our lives?

Another implication is to understand that the purpose of salvation is to restore us in our relationship with our creator. Consequently, while political liberation (to which some have reduced the exodus), economic justice or physical healing may serve as reflections of God's justice and useful models of salvation, they are not what Christianity teaches salvation to be unless they bring about a genuine reconciliation with God. To what extent have we secularised our understanding of salvation? How far do we mistake political, economic and social liberation for true salvation?

A third implication is to grasp the inability of us human beings to rescue ourselves and God's astonishing grace in doing so when we have done nothing to deserve it. This implication might lead to worship and to expressing our joyful gratitude to God for his great salvation, through prayer, through Holy Communion, through meditating on scriptures such as Exodus 15 or Ephesians 2:1–10, or through the use of a hymn such as 'Amazing Grace'.

1 Salvation as restoring God's rule

Mark 1:1–15

Jesus' first public words were to announce the arrival of God's reign, introducing a theme that was to govern his mission throughout. Israel, in theory, had acknowledged God to be their king. His sovereignty, not only over them but over the whole world, was much celebrated in their worship, as Psalms 72 and 93—100 illustrate. In reality, they had rejected his rule to a greater or lesser extent and lived under alien governance in what C.S. Lewis described as 'enemy occupied territory' (*Mere Christianity*, Fontana Books, 1955, p. 47). The evidence of enemy occupation was everywhere to be seen in the ruined and oppressed lives people lived. At last, Jesus claimed, with his arrival God was reclaiming his territory, liberating his people and bringing them back under his legitimate and beneficial rule.

God's rule was to be re-established in a surprising way. It was not to be restored in the expected way, through force and the crude imposition of power, but rather by the opposite means. God's agent was to bear the ills of the world by surrendering himself to the forces of evil, permitting them to do their worst, only for them to be completely defeated through his death and resurrection in the end. Jesus fits the description of Isaiah's servant exactly, bringing justice to the nations even though he didn't even raise his voice (Isaiah 42:1–3). No wonder C.S. Lewis went on in the quotation above to say that in Jesus 'the rightful king has landed, *you might say landed in disguise*'.

What's important here is that the concept of the kingdom of God is not different from the idea of salvation. God's rule frees people from the illegitimate powers with whom they've conspired, to their detriment, and brings them under his rule or, as Paul says later, 'into the kingdom of the Son he loves' (Colossians 1:13). Furthermore, this salvation is inextricably tied up with the coming of Jesus. He alone can defeat the enemy and rescue people, bringing them back under their rightful sovereign. As in any war, this calls for people to make a choice about which side they're on. So Jesus invites people 'to repent and believe the good news' (v. 15). The question is whether we're happy under alien rule or whether we line up with Jesus and his mission, costly though that may be.

2 Salvation as healing

Mark's gospel is particularly alert to the conflict between Satan's illegitimate occupation of the world and the rule of God. Early on he catalogues various ways in which Satan's influence in the world is malign, leading to disasters (4:35–41), demon-possession (5:1–20), disease (5:21–34), death (5:35–43) and a rejection of God's messenger (6:1–6). But the conflict between Satan and Jesus is triggered even before Mark details examples of our broken world.

No sooner had Jesus called a group together to be his companions than he visited the synagogue in Capernaum, which was initially to be the centre of his operations. Lay people were usually invited to preach in the synagogues, so there's nothing special about the invitation to Jesus to do so. But as soon as he opened his mouth, the congregation knew this man was different. Despite his youth, he spoke with conviction and authority and put a new spin on the old, familiar scriptures. The listeners were far from passive. Among them one became disruptive as inner demons made him cry out in opposition. The demons identified Jesus as more than the local boy made good, but rather as 'the Holy One of God!', a title only used previously of Samson (Judges 16:17; often translated 'Nazirite' in this verse). The demons were quickly, and spectacularly, despatched by Jesus and the man given back his humanity. The cosmic battle between Jesus and Satan had been joined, and Jesus had been revealed to be 'the strong man' (see Mark 3:27) who could rob Satan of his victims.

From then on, numerous exorcisms and healings followed. Jesus showed himself to be the superior power, restoring people to wholeness, the life God intended when he created them.

In the gospels, the word 'salvation' is used of deliverance from a whole range of troubles, but especially of exorcisms and physical healings (e.g. Mark 3:2; 5:28, 34; 6:56; 10:52), as well as healing from the inner sickness of sin which blights all humankind (Matthew 1:21). Physical healing was a significant sign of God's salvation and, given that Jesus viewed people as a unity, not as composed of isolated compartments, salvation that started in one aspect of life affected all the others too. So healing becomes 'a remarkably rich metaphor' for the outworking of salvation (Joel Green, *Why Salvation?*, Abingdon Press, 2013, p. 47).

3 Salvation as atonement

With John's gospel we enter a different world. Reflecting deeply on the mean-ing of Christ's mission, John gives us a different slant on Jesus than his fellow gospel writers. It was once common to claim that John taught that salvation was brought about by the incarnation of Jesus, rather than by his death and resurrection. A more balanced view now recognises that the gospel frequently teaches Christ atones for sin through his death and resurrection, even if the allusions to the cross are more imaginative than direct. For example, Jesus speaks of his body as a temple to be destroyed and rebuilt (2:18–19), the need to eat his flesh and drink his blood (6:53–58), the good shepherd laying down his life for the sheep (10:11) and the necessity of his being 'lifted up' (12:32–33).

In fact, John establishes that salvation will come through the atoning death of Christ from the start. John the Baptist twice announces that Jesus is 'the Lamb of God, who takes away the sin of the world' (1:29, 36), drawing on rich Old Testament imagery of the lamb. Scholars argue as to whether it was the Passover lamb, the lamb of Isaiah 53 or another sacrificial lamb which John had in mind. Certainty is not possible but, given that John replays the theme in some depth when reporting the crucifixion, it makes sense to see it as the Passover lamb. John's timescale differs from the other gospels to highlight that Jesus was sentenced to death at noon on 'the day of Preparation of the Passover' (19:14), the very moment the Passover lambs would have been slaughtered. Other elements of the Passover meal, described in Exodus 12, are echoed at the cross, like the mention of the hyssop plant and that none of his bones were broken.

Discussing the lamb's identity shouldn't divert us from focusing on the purpose of its sacrifice. The lamb's death 'takes away the sin of the world'. Just as surely as the refuse collectors remove the rubbish from our homes and streets, taking it far away from us, or the shower drains our dirt down the plughole, so Jesus gets rid of our sin and its consequences. He does so in the same way the Passover lamb led to Israel's deliverance: at the cost of his own life.

4 Salvation as grace

While some are doubtful if Paul personally wrote Ephesians, there can be no more classic expression of his doctrine of salvation than that found in today's reading. A short note cannot possibly do justice to the impressive theology here, where every phrase matters, but we can grasp the outline.

Paul (as we will refer to the author) begins with a statement of the problem which makes salvation necessary (vv. 1–3). Human beings are spiritually dead in relation to God as a result of the influence of their world, which is in rebellion against God because it is governed by God's enemy, the devil. Their own weak and corrupted constitutions, called 'the flesh', are of no help. All this puts them on the wrong side of God.

God's character, however, causes him to step in and make a way for spiritually dead people to come alive again (vv. 4–7). This is not reluctantly wrung out of him, for by nature his love is 'great' and he is 'rich in mercy'. The means through which God chose to make humans alive again is by uniting them with his Son, the Messiah, who entered into their death but is now resurrected, alive, never to die again and ruling from God's throne.

Paul is especially concerned for his readers – both Jews and Greeks – to grasp that this salvation is nothing people can earn or merit (vv. 8–9). It is a result of grace, of undeserved love, which can only be received as people believe God's promise. No one, whatever their religious heritage, can claim to have merited God's salvation. It is entirely a gift due to 'the incomparable riches of his grace'.

Paul is just as clear about the purpose of God's grace as he is about its means (vv. 9–10). Those who exercise faith and come alive in Christ do so that they might live transformed lives, characterised by good works, and become a new united humanity (vv. 11–22). Paul's words hint that this is a reassertion of God's intention at creation for humans. God's initial gift is in no way influenced by our spiritual status to start with, but in receiving the gift by faith we enter into an obligation to live to please God, shaking off, with the aid of God's Spirit, the death-dealing influence of the world, the flesh and the devil.

5 Salvation as reconciliation

Romans 5:8–11; 2 Corinthians 5:11–21

When Paul announced the good news of salvation, he reached for numerous models from his world to convey its meaning. They were more than analogies; they spoke about what was actual in salvation. Three models stand out. Justification came from the law courts, whereby someone was judged not guilty and put back in a right relationship with those who'd been offended. Redemption was taken from Israel's experience of slavery in Egypt and the contemporary slave market, whereby a price was paid for a slave's manumission. Reconciliation referred to warring factions overcoming their hostility and becoming friends. It applied as much to international conflicts as to family fallouts. While it isn't possible to separate reconciliation from Paul's other perspectives, many have argued that reconciliation is 'the heart of Paul's missionary theology' (e.g. Stanley Porter in *Paul as Missionary*, Trevor Burke and Brian Rosner (eds), T & T Clark, 2012, pp. 169–79).

The main outline of reconciliation is clear from today's readings. First, a state of enmity exists between us and God because of our sin. Second, the initiative in overcoming that state is taken by God, 'while we were still sinners' and his 'enemies'. He does this as an outworking of his love. As the offended party, overcoming the offence begins with him. Third, he overcomes it not by ignoring it but by dealing with it. Reconciliation occurs because his Son, who was entirely without fault, took upon himself our sin and its consequences, resulting in his death on the cross. Fourth, his death makes a totally transformative new beginning possible. People are made friends again with God. Their life now participates in the life of the risen Christ. Living righteously becomes an ambition and a possibility. And all this is a sign of the cosmic new creation to come. Finally, we become ambassadors of this good news, bringing it to those who've yet to hear or believe it, appealing to them to do so.

One detail calls for attention. Paul writes, 'God was reconciling the world to himself in Christ' (2 Corinthians 5:19). Does that mean that eventually all will be reconciled to God, regardless of how they've lived or whether they've believed? Is he advocating an automatic, universal salvation? No. As exegetes explain, in context Paul is using 'the world' as a synonym for 'we' and 'us'. Consequently, he appeals to them not to take God's reconciliation for granted but to pursue it by faith.

6 Salvation as re-creation

Revelation 21:1–8; 22:1–5, 12–21

A common misunderstanding of 2 Corinthians 5:17 makes it very personal: 'If anyone is in Christ they are a new creation.' While true, it's not what Paul said, nor is it his point. Referring to people being reconciled to God (and so to each other), Paul claims this is evidence of a new creation to come: 'the new creation has come'. The Christian vision of salvation is not that a few individuals will be rescued from a doomed earth to enjoy eternal bliss in heaven with God, but that the ultimate goal is the re-creation of heaven and earth so that they are restored to, and indeed surpass, God's original design.

How do you express such a vision? One way is to strain existing language and stretch existing experience to the limits to envisage what this future will be like. That's what John does at the end of Revelation, bringing the story of the Bible full circle. The story began with God living harmoniously among his creatures, free from the evil which would mar it. Due to the wilfulness of humankind, however, this original order gave way to disorder and to all manner of ills being inflicted on creation and humanity. But a totally new order of things will arrive, that of a recreated heaven and earth. In it, God will resume his place at the very heart of his people. Destructive forces will be banished from the cosmos. The abundant fruitfulness of the earth will be restored. The willing, obedient service of God will be resumed. God's reign will be re-established, beneficially, his throne being central to the community. The needs of humankind will be met from the bounty of the all-sufficient God. Salvation will have the final word.

Revelation teaches that this is not a disconnected act from what has gone before, but rather the final act of a work already in process. A breakthrough was reached in the first coming of Jesus, whose life, death and resurrection definitively altered the direction of our history. Satan was unquestionably defeated and deliverance from his reign of terror set in train. Yet, that work is not yet complete. It remains to be consummated, as it will be when the same Jesus comes again. Then salvation will be complete.

Until then, we pray, 'Amen. Come Lord Jesus.'

Guidelines

Paul neatly voiced a dilemma when he prayed that the Ephesians might 'grasp how wide and long and high and deep is the love of Christ, and to know this love that surpasses knowledge' (Ephesians 3:18–19). On the one hand, he prays that they might confidently enter into something of the complex, immeasurable, multifaceted gift of salvation. On the other hand, he admits that such love is unfathomable and inexhaustible. But that doesn't stop us from making a start.

Our whistle-stop tour has merely given us a glimpse of some aspects of salvation. It's worth asking: what other aspects of salvation would you have included? How else would you have expressed the truth of God's rescue mission in Christ? And what are the practical implications of experiencing salvation? We cannot, for example, boast about salvation as reconciliation unless we understand that it leads to our being reconciled with people who are different from us (Ephesians 2:11–22) and becoming one new humanity with them, and reconciled to people with whom we have close, and therefore sometimes troublesome, relationships in the local church (2 Corinthians 5:11–21). As you seek, from your own knowledge and experience, to broaden your understanding of salvation, make sure you anchor your thoughts in the Bible. What other passages or themes would you have latched on to? Otherwise you are in danger of drifting hazardously on the currents of your own imagination, instead of sailing in the surer waters of God's revelation.

Above all, keep the reason for Paul's prayer for the Ephesians central in your thinking. The purpose of exploring Christ's unfathomable love is not so that we can engage in theological argument but in humble worship. Our study of salvation will have failed unless, with Paul, we too 'kneel before the Father' in adoration at his amazing grace.

FURTHER READING

John Barclay, *Paul and the Subversive Power of Grace* (Grove Books, 2016).

Joel Green, *Why Salvation?* (Abingdon Press, 2015).

Derek Tidball, *The Voices of the New Testament: A conversational approach to the message of good news* (IVP, 2016).

Matthew 11—14

Andy Angel

Jesus began his ministry by proclaiming the nearness of the coming kingdom, which will start with God's judgement before he restores his people and fulfils his promises to them. Jesus went on to teach how all those who follow God should live. He has healed many and cast out countless demons. He has begun to challenge the people of God with the uncomfortable notion that they must respond to him and his message if they are to respond to God, and, if they fail to do this, sinners and Gentiles will enter the kingdom of heaven instead of them. He has also trained his disciples for mission so that they can go through all Israel before the day that the Lord comes to judge his people.

In the following chapters, Jesus continues his ministry of healing, exorcism and teaching. Not all respond to his call: some set themselves against him; others enjoy the healing but fail to respond to the call to repent; others follow him. Through all of this, Matthew explores who this Jesus really is who some are accepting and others are rejecting – and still others are only accepting in so far as they like parts of him. From his intimate prayer to the Father (11:25–27) to his walking on the water (14:22–33), Matthew shows us all that Jesus is the Son of God and uniquely identified with and as God himself. He reveals to us that we should accept in full, repent and learn from him how to live according to his teachings. Then we will understand who he truly is and what it means to call him Lord.

I am translating the Greek text myself in the studies below but recommend that you refer to the NRSV.

1 Confusion and a question

Matthew 11:2–6

When John baptised Jesus, it seems that he knew Jesus was the 'coming one' (Matthew 3:11–17), so you could be forgiven for wondering why John now sends his disciples to ask Jesus whether or not he is the 'coming one'. Even more intriguing is that John asks this question having heard about the works that Jesus is doing. John doubts that Jesus is the Messiah, and even if this seems strange to us, John has good reason. He is expecting the Messiah to come and judge the nation, to save the righteous and punish the wicked (Matthew 3:10–12). Jesus has done none of this – yet.

Instead, Jesus seems to be fulfilling the prophecies of the restoration of Israel. His words in verses 5–6 recall the prophecies of Isaiah 26:19 ('your dead shall live, their bodies shall rise'), Isaiah 29:18 ('the deaf shall hear'), Isaiah 35:5–6 ('the blind shall see' and 'the lame shall leap') and Isaiah 61:1 ('the poor have good news proclaimed'). However, all of the prophecies cited or alluded to talk of these things happening on the day when God comes to judge the earth. John might not hear of the judgement yet, but the miracles that Jesus performs are the signs that accompany the judgement of God.

There is even a hint of this in Jesus' rather enigmatic final words: 'Blessed is the person who does not take offence at me.' At one level, Jesus might be rebuking John: 'Read the signs and do not be offended that I am bringing salvation to people – judgement is surely coming.' At another level, Jesus hints more widely to all people that they should make sure their response to him is right. If these are the signs that he has come to judge, then people need to be right with him, as he will surely judge them. Jesus' response is as double-edged today as it was then. His signs and wonders, his transformations of lives and communities, are signs that he is the God of justice, that he will come again to judge the living and the dead. At the same time, he is the God in whom healing and restoration may be found.

2 John and a twist in the tale

Matthew 11:7–15

Jesus now asks the crowd to think about why they were so keen to see John the Baptist. They certainly did not go into the desert to look at the plant life or to find a rich fashion victim. They wanted to see John because they knew he was a prophet. But Jesus asks them to look more closely at exactly what place in God's story of salvation John held.

In answering the question, Jesus refers back to the scriptures. First, he takes his hearers to Exodus 23:20–33, telling them that John now plays the part of the angel of the Lord who guarded the children of Israel as they made their way to the promised land. John and the angel of the Lord both point the people of God in the right direction, so that they find the salvation God has prepared for them. Jesus then points his audience to Malachi 4:4–5, comparing John to Elijah. According to this prophecy, Elijah would come before the day when the Lord comes to judge and prepare the people of God for that day by calling them to repentance and reconciliation with each other.

In his reply, Jesus drops a hint about the changing nature of salvation. Up until now, the kingdom of heaven came through violence, and the violent seized it. Certainly, throughout the narratives of the Exodus to literature around the time of Jesus (like the extracanonical Psalms of Solomon and the War Scroll from the Dead Sea Scrolls), there was a history of expectation that God would give his people the land promised to Abraham through military victory. The Jewish historian Josephus mentions civil unrest around the time of Jesus and sporadically until the Jewish revolt in AD66–70. In those two words 'until now', Jesus suggests that now the nature of the kingdom is changing. Later in the gospel, he will teach his disciples that the military figure of the messiah is now to die on a cross to conquer sin and welcome all into fellowship with God. So the kingdom is now for all, Jew and Gentile, and comes through self-sacrificial love. Given the tradition of hostility between Jew and Gentile, bringing this kingdom community into reality will take much self-sacrificial love on all sides.

3 Just like naughty children

Matthew 11:16–19

Having dropped a hint that the kingdom is not coming the way in which many of his Jewish contemporaries were expecting, Jesus now rebukes them in a fairly stiff critique. He compares them to children playing games in the street. Rather than playing football or 'cowboys and Indians' (let alone computer games), the children are playing 'weddings and funerals'. Some are pretending to play the flute, but the others will not do the wedding dance. Some are wailing a lament, but the others will not beat their breasts in mourning.

Jesus compares this generation to these children calling out. John the Baptist and Jesus will not play their game properly. They do not like the fact that John fasted from eating and drinking, and they claim that he is demon-possessed. Jesus (referring to himself as 'the Son of Man') says that they also do not like the fact that Jesus does not fast, and they claim that he is a glutton and a drunk, a friend of tax-collectors and sinners. They complain about Jesus and John just as the children do, because Jesus and John do not meet their expectations.

Then Jesus goes on to compare himself and John to the figure of Wisdom (see Proverbs 1—9), who calls the people of God out of unrighteousness to live out the ways of God. Just as Wisdom is justified by her works of calling people to righteousness, so Jesus and John cannot be criticised for calling people to repentance and into righteous living in the covenant community – however they fail to meet the exact expectations of some. Moreover, Jesus' work in miraculous healings ('her works' in verse 19 probably recalls 'the works of the Messiah' in verse 2) also makes clear who Jesus is and calls people to follow him. But the people prefer to stick with their own expectations.

It is as easy now as it was then to box Jesus into what we expect him to do and to be, rather than following his way – however much it fails to live up to our expectations. It is good to reflect from time to time on whether we ourselves follow the whole of the Jesus we find in the gospels or just the Jesus of our favourite stories and sayings.

4 Responding rightly to the signs of the kingdom

Matthew 11:20–24

Now Jesus moves on to full-blown prophetic warnings. He has clearly done many works of power in Bethsaida and in Capernaum – the miracles he reported to the disciples of John the Baptist in verse 2: the blind see, the lame walk, the lepers are cleansed, the deaf hear, the dead are raised and the poor hear the good news preached. These are all signs that Jesus is the coming Messiah. Jesus is the person John prophesied about. Jesus is the person who will, as Malachi prophesied, bring in the great and terrible day of the Lord when God comes to judge.

Having critiqued some of his contemporaries for moaning like children about the fact that he and John did not meet their expectations, he now tells them in very plain language where they stand before God. He uses paradigms of wicked cities from the Old Testament (Tyre, Sidon and Sodom) to make his point. If they had seen the miracles that he has done in Bethsaida and Capernaum, they would have repented long ago. On the day when God judges the living and the dead, these notoriously wicked cities will have a much easier time of it that Capernaum and Bethsaida.

There is something slightly odd about all this that gives the clue to what Jesus really wants by way of response. The people of Bethsaida and Capernaum may see themselves as having accepted Jesus. After all, clearly many of them (and possibly those who live near them) have turned up to see Jesus. They have brought out their sick and demon-possessed, and Jesus has done many mighty miracles among them. If all Jesus came for was to heal and restore, then one might wonder why Jesus thinks they are worthy of great judgement. The reason is simple: Jesus first and foremost calls people to repentance, and he performs miracles so that people can see he is the Messiah and so repent. This is the only way they can join his people and enter the kingdom of heaven, and this is what he wants above all.

5 Knowing God

Matthew 11:25-27

Jesus now prays to the Father. Although the change of addressee seems abrupt, his prayer continues the theme that has been developing throughout chapter 11. Jesus reassured John the Baptist that he was the coming Messiah, as the miracles he has been performing demonstrated. He told the people that John is the prophet who came to lead God's people to salvation and to announce the great and terrible day of God's judgement. He indicated that the kingdom is not as some are expecting it to be, and he went on to rebuke those who rejected himself and John for not meeting their expectations. The he pronounced judgement on two towns who saw and enjoyed the miracles, but failed to see their significance and so did not repent as the Messiah warned them of the coming judgement.

Now Jesus blesses the Father for having concealed 'these things' from the wise and understanding and having revealed them to babes. Contextually, 'these things' must be the things about which Jesus has been speaking: his miracles being signs that he is the coming Messiah and John being the one who proclaimed him as Messiah, although many of his contemporaries do not see either of these things and respond appropriately.

It is always difficult to read of God concealing truth from people, and it raises the question why. In this context, it is not because Jesus has not proclaimed the gospel and healed them, just as he has with everyone everywhere that he has been so far. In Jesus, God has reached out to all. Perhaps the contrast is that God has shown his ways to the spiritually weak ('babes' most likely refers to those who seem less likely to have religious or spiritual understanding).

Jesus' final words in these verses reveal the intimacy of his relationship with the Father. They also reveal that humanity has a propensity not to recognise God – as only the Father recognises the Son and vice versa. The only exception is where the Son reveals to people the person and nature of the Father. Perhaps, as we listen to these words, we should find ourselves falling to our knees and asking the Son to reveal the person and nature of the Father and of himself, the Son, in our generation.

12–18 October

51

6 'Come unto me'

Matthew 11:28–30

Jesus now invites his audience into this relationship with God. However, this relationship is one not simply of knowing or feeling the presence of God, but of listening to and learning from the Son, so that he might work his transforming power in our lives and characters. His call here cannot be a call to lay down burdens (in the sense of problems), as he calls people to take up his burden and yoke. If it were a call to lay down our problems, then his response of giving us some more is not very kind.

Jesus uses the term 'yoke' to mean the law. Rabbis spoke of 'the yoke of the law'. Jesus speaks of the Pharisaic interpretation of the law as 'burdens' (23:4), which they impose on people without helping them. To be clear and to avoid hypocrisy, the Pharisees built a hedge around the law to help people not break God's commands. That is, they had a code which they recommended people stick to which would help them not to come anywhere near breaking God's commands, because breaking those commands puts one out of relationship with God. To be fair, the Pharisees' motivation to stay pure before God is biblical and laudable. Moreover, many Christians do exactly the same thing, not least in giving pastoral advice, and so ought to be wary of criticising the Pharisees too readily.

Jesus speaks into the situation of those who are exhausted trying to follow God by keeping his commands and trying to follow the codes of the Pharisees. He tells them to take his 'yoke', or law or teaching, upon them and learn from him. He is a gentle and humble teacher who comes alongside us and teaches us as we can learn – rather than telling us that we fail if we do not hit his programme targets. We could all do well to turn to Jesus, not only to learn obedience to his teachings ourselves but also to learn his grace and gentleness, for without that our attempts to teach or nurture people in the faith fail to represent Jesus as he truly is. He is the one teacher and we can only teach about him in grace and love.

Guidelines

What might seem like disparate stories threaded together in chapter 11 form a remarkably coherent unit. What binds them together is their fundamental challenge: you have seen the signs that Jesus has done, which fulfil the prophetic expectations of the Messiah and the age he will usher in; what is your response? The age will not come in without God's first judging all the nations, including his own people. This makes sense: nothing unholy can enter God's kingdom, as God is utterly holy and will live among his people. Therefore, if there is anything unholy or impure in our lives, we must repent.

There is quite a contemporary edge to this chapter. Churches have become so keen to be relevant to the culture into which they speak that they have too easily reduced 'the kingdom of God' to the blessings that God will bestow in the kingdom. They confuse the signs of the kingdom with the kingdom itself – whether they are miracles or the transformation of societies (or both). But as Jesus' critique of Bethsaida and Capernaum shows, this is far from true. The miracles are to draw us to repentance so that on the day he comes to judge, Jesus will welcome us into the kingdom. This confusion reduces the kingdom from the establishment of justice to the doling out of benefits. By failing to recognise the gospel as Jesus teaches it, the Father becomes an indulgent aunt rather than a holy, good and forgiving God – and our worship turns towards idolatry as we do not worship God as he truly is.

But the punch really comes in Matthew 11:27. We can so fail to see God for all the benefits we would rather have, or the visions we have created for ourselves of what God should be like, that we simply do not know God. We can only know the Father as Jesus reveals him. For us today, this means through scripture, as the gospels contain Jesus' words and actions and so inform us of who he is and what he does. However, as verse 29 reveals, this cannot be limited to learning the book and believing it; it must also include the personal relationship with the living Lord Jesus, who alone can bring the book to life and have us meet with God.

1 Sabbath controversy

Matthew 12:1–14

In the two stories we have read, Jesus finds himself at odds with the Pharisees. However, the reason for the conflict between them is not, as is often suggested, one of love verses law – as if love liberated us from moral commands. Jesus does not break the law, and nor do his disciples. The law does state that you shall do no work on the sabbath (Exodus 20:8–11) and that you shall not harvest on the sabbath (Exodus 34:21) – but the disciples are not harvesting; they are simply plucking the odd ear of corn to eat. They are not breaking any command in the law. Neither does Jesus break any commandment when he heals on the sabbath, because there is no commandment in the law that says you shall not heal on the sabbath.

Why, then, are the Pharisees accusing Jesus of doing what is not lawful? We know from later writings (Jerusalem Talmud, tractate Shabbat 7:2) that the Pharisees debated whether it would be wise to prohibit plucking any corn on the sabbath to stop anyone getting anywhere near breaking the command not to harvest on the sabbath. We also know that the Pharisees were discussing how much healing might be allowed on the sabbath, as they ruled it was permitted to heal when life was in danger (Mishnah, tractate Yoma 8:6). As we have seen, the Pharisees added many commands to those in the law so as to prevent people from breaking it.

So Jesus' disagreement with the Pharisees is not about whether God's commandments ought to be obeyed; it is about whether the Pharisees' additional commandments ought to be obeyed, and Jesus clearly sees no reason to endorse or obey them. Jesus does not criticise the law here. In fact, earlier in the gospel he stresses the importance of obeying God's commands (5:17–20). Immediately after teaching his disciples to take his yoke (his teaching or law) upon themselves, Jesus shows them by his own example what they do not need to follow. For those exhausted by following the Pharisees, this was very important. Perhaps for us today in the libertarian western world, it is more important that we relearn the importance of coming to Jesus, our teacher, to learn from him how to obey his commands.

2 Jesus the servant

As the Pharisees plot against Jesus, he withdraws from those parts and carries on his ministry elsewhere. As they have done consistently up to this point, the crowds follow him and he heals them. He also rebukes them not to make him known. There are various points in the gospels where Jesus tells others not to make him known. Not surprisingly, people have asked why he did this. The question has given rise to much scholarly speculation and even full-blown theses about 'the messianic secret'. Nowadays, scholars are more circumspect and wonder if there were different reasons for requiring silence on different occasions. Possibly here, Jesus does not want the Pharisees catching up with him – after all, they were plotting to kill him.

Whatever the reason, Matthew sees this as fulfilling the scripture that comes in the middle of his quotation: 'He will not quarrel or contend, nor will anyone hear his voice in the plazas' (v. 19). He has withdrawn from the Pharisees rather than continue the controversy with them. This quotation from Isaiah 42:1–4 serves Matthew well, as it highlights many aspects of Jesus' life and ministry which Matthew seeks to illustrate in the gospel. The first few lines remind us of what happened at Jesus' baptism: God revealed that Jesus was his beloved Son, with whom he was very pleased, and the Spirit came upon him. The opening lines of Jesus' ministry, 'Repent for the kingdom of heaven is near', and his sending out of his disciples later in the gospel to make disciples of the nations fulfil this prophecy that 'he will announce judgement to the nations'. His 'not breaking a crushed wick or putting out a smouldering wick' speak of his compassion to the poor, weak and needy, among and to whom he constantly ministers throughout the gospel, not least in his ministry of healing, exorcism and preaching good news to the poor. 'The nations hope in his name' precisely because he not only includes those outside Israel and ministers to them (e.g. the centurion's son or servant), but he also sends his disciples to take his good news out to the ends of the earth.

Jesus' significance stretches across time and throughout the world. In the narrative, he could look like a wandering preacher sheltering from danger, but, in reality, he is the divine Son before whom all will bow the knee when he comes to judge the earth.

3 A controversy and a puzzle

Jesus performs a wonderful healing and the crowds are ecstatic. The Pharisees hear about it and try to work out how this might fit with their theology – after all, a man who does not accept their hedge around the Torah takes neither holiness nor God seriously. They conclude that he casts out demons by the power of the devil. This leads to an extended response from Jesus (vv. 25–37).

Part of Jesus' response is puzzling. Given that he clearly does not agree with the Pharisees' claim that his ministry is inspired by the devil, why would he claim that the kingdom of God has come upon them (v. 28)? This seems to make no sense in the context as by rejecting Jesus they are surely rejecting the kingdom of God. This is only partly true. From the kingship psalms (e.g. Psalm 97) onwards, the picture of the coming of the kingdom in Judaism was more or less like this: God comes in glory; he takes his throne to judge; he destroys the enemies of Israel; he punishes the wicked in Israel; and then he restores the righteous poor in Israel to an everlasting kingdom of holiness, prosperity and peace. The first thing that happens when the kingdom of God comes is that God comes in his glorious theophany to judge. When the kingdom comes, these Pharisees will be judged and, given their rejection of Jesus, the coming of the kingdom will not be good news for them.

The promise of the kingdom of God is not necessarily good news for everyone. It can mean life, health, peace and happiness in loving and worshipful relationship with the living God – or it can mean the punishment we deserve for all the bad things we have done towards ourselves and others and for our lack of worship of the one true God. Whether the kingdom of God is something to look forward to or not really depends on where we stand with God, and that requires each of us to respond appropriately to God's invitation to repent and be forgiven and filled with the Holy Spirit. As Jesus put it, 'Whoever speaks a word against the Son of Man will be forgiven; but whoever speaks against the Holy Spirit will never be forgiven, either in this world or the next' (v. 32).

4 'An evil and adulterous generation'

Now the scribes and the Pharisees ask for a sign. But why shouldn't the miracle that some of the Pharisees have just commented on act as a sign? After all, Jesus has already said that his healing the blind shows that he is the coming Messiah (11:5). These Pharisees seem to be trying to puzzle Jesus out. Perhaps they are not all convinced that he is empowered by Satan. On the other hand, they are not yet convinced he is the Messiah either.

Jesus' response speaks in a veiled way of the sufferings, death and resurrection he is about to undergo and which he will begin to tell his disciples about later. He quotes Jonah 2:1, perhaps with a certain ironic humour. (Why else compare his saving work on the cross with God's punishment of the least obedient prophet of the Jewish scriptures?) He compares the three days and nights Jonah spent in the monster (the Greek word means 'sea monster') with the time Jesus will spend in the tomb. Then he adds a twist. The Ninevites repented when this recalcitrant prophet Jonah preached to them. Now someone much greater than Jonah is preaching to this generation, and they will not listen and repent, so the Ninevites will rise up at the judgement and condemn them. This was radical teaching, as contemporary Jewish pictures of the judgement had the Jews rescued and restored and the Gentiles punished (e.g. 4 Ezra 13:25–50). Jesus then underlines the point by changing the cast: someone greater than Solomon is here and the Gentile Queen of Sheba will condemn this evil and adulterous generation. The right response to Jesus is to repent and follow him, not to question or judge him.

This passage ought to give us pause and question whether there is any complacency in our spiritual lives. Are we so content with our patterns of religious life and worship that we are quite happy not to seek further the truth of Jesus and more of his transforming work in our lives? Our mistakes may not be exactly the same as the Pharisees (building a hedge around the law – although many Christians do this in practice), but there may be sufficient similarities that it is time to think, repent and change our ways.

5 Jesus' family

This short story is as simple as it is shocking. Family ties were very close in ancient Israel. Tradition has it that Joseph died young, so Jesus, as eldest son, probably held responsibility for his family for a while – working as a craftsman (Greek *tektōn*, Mark 6:3). He has left home and passed on his responsibilities to earn money for the family, presumably, to younger siblings. They have come to visit him. Matthew does not mention their reasons, although in Mark we get the idea that they are worried about him (Mark 3:21, 31–35). Someone even tells Jesus that his mother and siblings are waiting outside for him – presumably so that he stops teaching and spends time with them. That would seem to be the appropriate response to a visit from the family.

Jesus may well have stopped and spent time with this family – the text does not tell us either way, and so we will never know. However, it does report something which is both shocking and beautiful. Before he even goes to greet his family, he asks who his family are. This must have been heard (at least, initially) as an insult to his family. He then turns to his disciples and says that they are his family: 'Whoever does the will of my Father in heaven is my brother and sister and mother' (v. 50). Again, possibly shocking, as it sounds as if he replaces his family (who appear to care for him) with other people.

On the other hand, he does not specify that his birth family are excluded, and later on we know they were right at the centre of the early community of disciples. So this is not a case of exclusion – quite the reverse is true. Jesus begins in his ministry the most radical inclusion of all relationships – treating all his disciples as his own closest relatives. His vision, and the reality that he wants to teach us to live out, is that we relate to each other with the most intimate of love. There is no place for isolation or loneliness in the church. We are to care for each other as we would our blood family. Blood is thicker than water, but the blood shed on the cross is thicker still.

6 The parable of the sower

Jesus tells his disciples that this parable is about sowing the word about the kingdom. This 'word' is Jesus' proclamation, 'Repent for the kingdom of heaven has drawn near' (4:17). So the parable concerns the proclamation that God will come again and judge. When he does, he will reward the righteous, punish the wicked and establish a kingdom of universal peace and justice. Addressing people Jesus knows to be sinful, he calls them to repentance – that is, turning from lives of sin to lives of righteousness, living as he has taught people to live.

The parable concerns people's responses. Some just do not understand, for whatever reason, and the 'evil one' takes the word right out of their hearts and minds. Some hear it and love what they hear, but not so much that they find it worthwhile to go through difficult times for the sake of their faith. For others, their worries about all the challenges in life and their desire to get rich strangles the faith out of them. These excuses have a remarkably contemporary ring and match what I see in pastoral ministry on a daily basis. Some people really cannot be bothered at all about faith or worship. Some really like the idea that God loves them utterly and unconditionally, but their own love for God will not cope with challenges. When these come, worship disappears, prayer disappears and they express disappointment in God as they cannot feel his love. Others are just too busy with work and leisure to make it; when not working to pay the mortgage, they are taking the kids to a park run. Jesus was and is no fool. He knew and knows an excuse when he sees one.

But others get it. They let the seed root deeply and they nurture it so it grows. They know their need of God, and their repentance is genuine. They may have their struggles with God and faith, but they continue. They also see God as their priority – and so the other things in life simply have to take their rightful place. These people bear fruit, both in the way they live and in their sharing of their faith.

Guidelines

In the readings for this week, Matthew has drawn particular attention to Jesus' arguments with the Pharisees, as he teaches that people are not required to obey all the extra commands they added to the law. Too often in recent decades, certain Christians have misunderstood Jesus' critique of the Pharisees. They have claimed that the Pharisees taught a religion of following the law (calling it 'legalism'), but that Jesus taught a religion of love instead. This is plain nonsense. The Pharisees also taught love, as the law commands that we love God (Deuteronomy 6:5) and love our neighbour as ourselves (Leviticus 19:18). And Jesus taught the same commands as the two greatest commandments, that is, instructions God has given in the law that we are to obey (Matthew 22:34–40). Jesus does not replace the law with love, but teaches that loving God and our neighbours is where obedience to his teaching begins.

This is important. Teaching that Jesus replaces the Pharisees' legalism with love is not just plain nonsense; it is pernicious nonsense. First, it misrepresents Jesus and teaches people to believe things he never said and that contradict his teachings. Second, it caricatures the Pharisees, perpetuating lies about them (and contemporary Jews), which Christians post-Holocaust should not want to do.

It also cuts people off from the salvation which Christ offers us. Jesus promised in Matthew 5:17 that he would fulfil the law and the prophets, that is, he would teach people how to live. He expands on that promise in Matthew 11:28–30, where he promises to teach people how to live out his law ('take my yoke upon you and learn from me') in humility and gentleness and with the strength to see us through. His vision for his disciples involves us becoming a community of humble people, who help and support each other in our growth into holiness without hypocrisy and with vulnerability, transparency and grace. He longs to nurture us as a people who seek his holiness in love and kindness. Current pseudo-gospels which relativise the importance of this sanctification for the sake of their message of unconditional acceptance, with little to no expectation of change, rob people of the hope and expectation that Jesus will be true to his word, enter into our lives and change us for the better.

1 The parable of the tares

Matthew 13:24–43

There are various myths doing the rounds about the kingdom of God, the best of which are half-truths. One is that the kingdom of God refers to the political transformation of society; another is that the kingdom of God refers to extraordinary works of the Holy Spirit, such as healing miracles and prophecies. These and other ideas (sometimes called 'realised eschatology') are generally rooted in Old Testament texts which explore the action of God as king. The parables of Jesus are often the place that people come to find a text which might justify their particular understanding of the kingdom. The parable of the tares is the gravedigger for all such interpretations of the kingdom.

There could not be a clearer statement from the lips of the Jesus in the gospels which identifies the kingdom of heaven with the day of judgement. The owner of the field is the Son of Man – that is, Jesus, in his earthly ministry, proclaiming repentance and the kingdom, teaching and healing. The enemy is the devil. The good seed are those who respond to Jesus. The tares are those who do not. The harvest is the end of the age. The angels are the harvesters. Everything that causes people to sin and every sinner will be weeded out and cast into the fire. The righteous will enter the kingdom of the Father. Elsewhere in the gospel we discover that in this kingdom God reigns in justice and society is transformed, and elsewhere in scripture we find that there will be no more suffering or pain. These things are parts of the kingdom, but only after God judges. This is the case throughout the scriptures: as we have seen, God comes in glory, judges from his throne, rewards the righteous, punishes the wicked and establishes peace and justice.

I came across a minister recently who gave a talk about judgement, spelling out the different eternal consequences of repenting and ignoring the offer of forgiveness. A member of their congregation commented that they did not think anyone did evangelism like this anymore. Given that Jesus did exactly this (in all of the four gospels), perhaps more of us should consider giving it a try.

2 Finding treasure

The first of these final parables speaks of a man who finds treasure hidden in a field. He quickly hides it again and then, overjoyed, goes to sell all he has to buy the field. The picture is simple and easy to imagine. Who would not be extremely happy if great wealth suddenly fell into their hands so easily? The financial calculation is relatively simple. What I currently possess is worth a small amount compared with the cash value of the treasure. What I have could pay for the field. If I own the field, I own the treasure. I make myself many times wealthier by selling what I have and buying that one field.

Perhaps there is more of a sting in the parable than we normally notice. Jesus has already taught his disciples not to store up treasure on earth, where moth and rust do their work, but instead to store up treasure in heaven (6:19–21). Later in the gospel, he will teach us that anyone who gives up houses or fields for him will receive 100 times as much, along with eternal life (19:29). Surely 100 times as much makes for a very sound investment. Current interest rates are unlikely to offer anything like this return (at least at the time of writing in the UK). Why, then, do we find this so much easier to talk about than to put into practice?

Perhaps this parable takes us right back to the parable of the sower and asks us to think again. Though seeking to follow Christ, are we not just a little bit like those who are overjoyed at the message but do not grow enough root to live it? Maybe there are parts of us which are overly concerned with our wealth and not concerned enough with giving up all we have to Jesus. The early church owned their property but with the mindset that it belonged to the church community, and they sold it when others were in need of the money it could raise (Acts 4:32–34). Perhaps we could all pray that the Spirit so transforms our minds and hearts that we all think and live that way in our churches today.

3 Cousins in rejection

Having collected together many of Jesus' parables and given further insights into his teaching about the kingdom, Matthew continues his narrative of Jesus' ministry. Just as he paired the story of the beginning of John's ministry by the Jordan with the beginning of Jesus' ministry, he now pairs the stories of the rejection of Jesus and John by various of their fellow countrymen. They began ministry with the same proclamation (3:2; 4:17) and now both face rejection. Herod beheads John, and this action foreshadows Jesus' own not-too-distant death – not least as the first thing John's disciples do after burying their master is to go and tell Jesus what has happened.

Also poignant is the rejection of Jesus by the people with whom he grew up. They know his mother and father, name his brothers and point to the fact that all his sisters are with them. To them, this seems reason enough for them to reject his teaching. Since the story of Jesus' baptism, Matthew has been signalling to the gospel audience that Jesus is not simply a teacher but the Son of God. This makes his old friends' rejection of him as a teacher more than a touch ironic for the gospel audience who are already in the know as to who Jesus really is.

Even more ironic is the final editorial comment in chapter 13, which also strikes a note of grace: 'And he did not do many miracles there on account of their lack of faith' (13:58). It would be easy to get caught up in discussing the role of faith in the recipients in healing ministry, but this would miss the point being made about God's generosity. The townsfolk dismiss Jesus. They do not have faith in him. We would expect to read 'Jesus did not perform *any* miracles', when in fact we read 'Jesus did not perform *many* miracles'. In other words, he did perform some. His grace is more powerful than our foolishness and lack of faith. It is also kinder, as Jesus is clearly willing to risk further disrespect by continuing his ministry in praying for the healing of some of the very people who are rejecting him. His love is more gracious than our ingratitude.

4 Feeding 5,000-plus

Matthew 14:13–21

There are at least two miracles in this story. The most obvious is that Jesus feeds 5,000 men and (presumably) their families with only five loaves and two fish. This miracle of multiplication can be seen most clearly in the fact that there are twelve large baskets of bits of food left over.

The second miracle is surely the faith of the disciples. Five thousand men, with women and children also, is an awful lot of people. If we guess that the men brought wives and a couple of children each, that is 20,000 mouths to feed. You can understand why the disciples suggest to Jesus that he sends the crowds off to find something to eat. This is common sense. They give another common-sense reply when Jesus tells them to give the crowds something to eat. The implication is quite clear: you cannot feed 5,000-plus people on five loaves of bread and two fish. However, they obey him all the same. They take him the bread and fish. When he breaks and blesses them, they take the pieces to the crowds. How must they have felt at that point? What was going through their minds? They could easily be forgiven for having thought that the food would not stretch and it would all end in embarrassment.

Stepping out in obedience to Jesus may not be easy. But the disciples found that Jesus could be trusted. Whether there were just over 5,000, 20,000 or more, Matthew states that all ate and were satisfied. Whatever happened as Jesus blessed and broke the bread and fish, and as the disciples passed them around, the food was multiplied. (Incidentally, rationalising explanations, such as suggesting that everyone took out their food and shared it round, simply add details to the story that are not there. Matthew tells us a miracle story, and we are meant to read it as such.)

Sometimes, like the disciples, Jesus asks us to do what we find impossible – whether this is something in his teaching we find hard to believe we can do or something which through prayer we believe the Lord has called us to do. In situations like these, we (like Jesus) need to look to heaven and then ask for the faith to step out and obey.

5 Walking on water

Matthew 14:22–33

In telling this now well-known story, Matthew draws on an ancient myth, which pictures God as a warrior, coming in the storm to defeat his enemies the chaos waters and the dragon (e.g. Psalm 18:4–15). The chaos waters and dragon symbolise the enemies of God's people, from nations that attack them to famine and death. God dries up the sea and splits the dragon in two. In one place, God walks on the back of the sea (pictured as a monster, Job 9:8). Matthew uses the words found in the Greek translation of this verse in the Septuagint when he talks of Jesus walking on the sea.

By quoting this verse, Matthew indicates that Jesus comes as the warrior God who can defeat the chaotic sea and the threat of death. However, the disciples think they see a ghost, and they are terrified. Jesus calls out to them not to be afraid and identifies himself with two Greek words which could mean 'It's me!' or 'I AM' (the name God gives himself in Exodus 3:14). So in words and actions Jesus has communicated to the disciples in the boat that he is the Lord of Hosts, the God who comes with the heavenly armies to rescue his people from chaos and death.

However, the disciples need more persuading before they can believe. Peter makes a stunning reply: 'If you are…' He turns the divine name 'I AM' into a question, 'ARE YOU?', as he requests that Jesus demonstrates he really is the Lord who rescues from chaos and death. A few moments later, Peter walks on the waters. (Incidentally, Jesus walks on the 'sea' but Peter walks on the 'waters', so that we do not confuse Peter with God in Job 9:8.) Then Peter doubts and begins to drown and cries out to Jesus to save him. This Jesus does immediately and rescues him from the chaos waters and death, proving that he is God the warrior, the Lord of Hosts.

Peter gets too much flack. His example is wonderful. He has the courage to give God a go, take him seriously and step out in faith. He also has the courage to call out for help when he makes his mistake in taking his eyes off Jesus. And his faith brings faith to the other disciples.

6 Extraordinary miracles

Matthew 14:34–36

Despite the conflicts and the questions, this summary statement of Jesus' ministry still pictures him as remarkably popular as a healer. As soon as he has crossed over the other side of the lake, people recognise him, and the word goes around the whole of that region that Jesus is there. People bring all their sick and even beg him just to touch the fringe of his garment, because all those who have even this minimal contact with him are healed.

The small detail of the fringe of his garment tells us something important – not least in preparation for the next story, in which Jesus and the Pharisees come into some conflict over the interpretation of the law. (Note that Jesus expects the Pharisees to obey the fifth commandment, 'Honour your father and your mother', properly, so as we have seen he cannot be teaching that the law is replaced by love.) The law commands Jewish men to wear fringes or tassels on their garments (Deuteronomy 22:12). The tassels were to be worn to remind people of all the commandments of the Lord so that they would do them (Numbers 15:38–39). Jesus wore fringes or tassels in his clothing, which means that he was observing these commandments; these fringes were there to remind Jesus to obey all God's commands. Jesus was not a preacher of love instead of the law. Even the clothing he wore shows his commitment to obedience to God's commands.

This ought to keep us alert as we move into the next story and make us wary of any reading which suggests that Jesus broke the law or taught others to do the same (not least as sometimes people have interpreted Matthew 15:1–20 and its parallel in Mark 7:1–23 this way). It prepares us to read the conflict clearly and carefully and note, as we have before, that Jesus' conflict with the Pharisees was over their additional teachings. Jesus only requires that we obey God's commands, and this we find above all in his own teaching.

Guidelines

Stepping out in faith has become something of a cliché, but I think it contains a very important truth for all who profess Christian faith. There are times when we will find ourselves swimming against the tide of society, or even against contemporary trends within parts of the church. Being willing to follow Christ whatever the cost is fundamental to true Christian faith. We can settle all too easily for shades of grey in our commitment to Christ. The stories this week highlight some of the areas in which we might fall foul of this temptation.

Money can easily become a problem. I hear far more people nowadays talking of how we can give time or expertise instead of money, and that honouring what people are able to give is important. True. We can give time and expertise, and honouring each other in all things is always important. But Jesus himself taught both tithing (Matthew 23:23) and giving to the poor on top of this (6:2–4). I think that many of us contemporary western Christians still struggle with 'selling everything we have' to buy that field and invest our treasures in the kingdom of heaven.

Obeying Jesus can also feel threatening. We can find much of our security in ourselves, and sometimes Jesus commands us to do things which take us out of ourselves. This might be some aspect of his teaching which we find hard because we are going to have to change our patterns of behaviour or worship. Alternatively, it might be some new ministry we believe he is calling us to do, which we have discerned in prayer and tested with wise fellow disciples. Whatever the challenge, it requires us to change our lives, sometimes to be changed as people, and this leaves us uncomfortable.

So perhaps we all ought to take another look at Peter. He may not have been perfect – as many preachers have been happy to point out down the ages. However, he certainly trusted Jesus enough to give him a go and see what happened. He got out of the boat and walked on water. He also relied on Jesus when things went wrong. He cried out to him when he started to sink. His example of turning to Christ with his faltering and questioning faith is one worth emulating.

FURTHER READING

Andy Angel, *The Jesus You Really Didn't Know: Rediscovering the teaching ministry of Jesus* (Cascade, 2019).

R.T. France, *The Gospel of Matthew* (Eerdmans, 2007).

Daniel J. Harrington, *The Gospel of Matthew* (Liturgical Press, 1991).

Contemporary scholarship 20:20

Helen Morris

> What has been will be again, what has been done will be done again; there
> is nothing new under the sun.
> ECCLESIASTES 1:9

In these notes I will be exploring areas in which contemporary scholarship
has significantly changed or enhanced our understanding. The quotation
from Ecclesiastes 1:9 probably seems an odd way to introduce this theme.
Moreover, the Teacher's point seems verifiably false; he did not tweet it, for
example! New technology is regularly developed, and contemporary scholars
write new things about ancient, yet living, biblical texts. However, such new
developments do not actually contradict or challenge the Teacher's meaning,
for he speaks in wisdom of a deeper truth. There is constancy to the created
world: in every era the sun rises and sets, children play, birds fly, people get
angry, excited, happy, hungry and sad. This constancy in creation reflects the
constancy of the creator, 'who does not change like shifting shadows' (James
1:17). However, although God's character never changes, our knowledge of
him can. Our eyesight can sharpen so that we see through the dim glass more
clearly. Our understanding of scripture can grow, and sometimes be challenged
and changed. New treasures can come out of the storeroom as well as old.

The area of contemporary scholarship that I will focus on this week is the trend
towards literary approaches to scripture. The notion that the Bible is literature
is neither new nor newsworthy (the Teacher's words are apt again). However,
while questions of historical reliability were prominent in 20th-century biblical
scholarship, in recent years the emphasis has moved to literary criticism: an
analysis of the text's language with attention to, for example, the author's use
of metaphor, repetition, word choice and wordplays. I will address two areas
in particular: narrative criticism (paying attention to how the author relays a
particular story and why they recount it in this way) and rhetorical criticism
(examining what effect in the reader the author wanted to create and to what end).

Unless otherwise stated, Bible quotations are taken from the NIV.

1 Beating bitterness

Genesis 4:1–16

In the 1980s, Robert Alter argued that literary analysis – 'attention to the artful use of language' – was still in its infancy (*The Art of Biblical Narrative*, p. 12). To illustrate its usefulness, he analyses the insertion of Judah and Tamar's story into the Joseph account (Genesis 38). He notes how Jacob's refusal to be comforted (37:35) contrasts with the brevity of Judah's mourning before he sleeps with Tamar (38:12), and how Judah, the deceiver of his father through the blood of a young goat (37:31), becomes the deceived in a deception that, likewise, involves a young goat (38:17, 20–22). There is no explicit condemnation of Judah; it is the contrasts that reveal the narrator's assessment. The resulting negative portrayal is significant, given that God's intervention through Joseph serves to preserve the messianic line that comes from Judah's indiscretion. God chooses unlikely people to progress his plans.

The apparent arbitrariness of God's election arises, too, in Cain and Abel's story. R.W.L. Moberly highlights parallels with Jacob and Esau to argue that, just as the divine favouring of Jacob over Esau occurs in the womb, before any actions are performed (Genesis 25:23), so God's favouring of Abel's sacrifice over Cain's is just that, favouring (*The Theology of the Book of Genesis*, CUP, 2009, pp. 88–101). Sin crouches at Cain's door after the sacrifice is rejected, not before; the lesson is not 'make sure you offer the best sacrifice', but 'how will you respond when others seem more favoured than you?'

Esau's relenting of his murderous intent and welcome of Jacob (in language that prefigures the Father's embrace of the prodigal son) shows that he defeats the devouring beast of bitterness (33:4). Cain does not, and resonance with Genesis 3 emphasises his fall. 'Where is your brother?' (4:9) mirrors the 'Where are you?' of Genesis 3:9. Cursing of the ground and exclusion from it appear in both accounts (3:23; 4:16).

What light does this literary analysis shed? Attention to 'the artful use of language' highlights the following: God is good but sometimes acts in ways we do not understand or which even seem unfair. This can tempt us to doubt his goodness, leading to sin, which damages relationships and leads to exclusion. God's response demonstrates his grace (3:20–21; 4:15): life is preserved and, even through people like Judah, God outworks his redemptive plans.

2 Motivated by models

If you created a new superhero, what superpower would they have? What would they do and not do? What characteristics would they display?

I don't know what superhero came to mind for you, but I assume that they are strong, wear some kind of costume, rescue people and defeat baddies. I can presume these things because I've watched superhero films and, over time, developed a model (or paradigm) of what a superhero is and does.

Waldemar Janzen argues that something similar occurs when we read Old Testament narratives (*Old Testament Ethics: A paradigmatic approach*, John Knox Press, 1994). As we read story after story of those faithful (and unfaithful) to God, we build up a picture of what God's people are meant to look like (and not look like). That none of these characters is perfect is no barrier; increasingly, superheroes are presented as flawed in contemporary film. Subtle, and unsubtle, narrative clues help us recognise behaviour and attitudes we are to aspire to and those we should seek to avoid. For instance, by the time we have read about Esau's susceptibility to Jacob's deception because of his lust for food (Genesis 25:29–34), Jacob's susceptibility to Laban's deception because of his lust for Rachel (Genesis 29:1–30) and Shechem's susceptibility to Jacob's sons' deception because of his lust for Dinah (Genesis 34:1–31), we begin to notice a pattern. Lust leads to folly.

By way of positive example, in Ruth, an Israelite (Boaz) and a Moabite (Ruth) provide models of good living that inspire emulation: Ruth's loyalty to Naomi and, crucially, to Naomi's God; Boaz's care for the stranger and widow. People inspire us more than principles. Identifying biblical axioms (be just, be righteous, be loving, etc.) is important. But seeing such characteristics in action in the (albeit imperfect) men and women of scripture better enthuses our attempts to live as God's people today.

3 Looking up and out

Job starts with a challenge set by the Accuser, 'the Satan'. Does Job fear God for nothing (1:9)? Does he worship God for God himself or just for his gifts? God accepts the challenge, and the Accuser is allowed to afflict Job, who has no idea of the conversation that precedes his suffering. Given this start, one might expect the book to finish with a triumphal God informing the Accuser that, though Job expressed much ill feeling in his lament, he did not 'curse God to his face', as the Accuser had predicted (1:11). But, contrary to the reader's expectations, the Accuser does not appear again. Instead, after several rounds of dialogue between Job and his friends, God appears in a whirlwind, not to answer Job's questions but to ask some of him: 'Where were you when I laid the earth's foundation?… Who shut up the sea behind doors?… Have you ever given orders to the morning?' (38:4, 8, 12).

Robert Alter demonstrates the value of close attention to the dialogue's detail (*The Art of Biblical Poetry*, pp. 119–20). He highlights the contrast between Job's lowly laments and God's grand elocutions. Job's laments go down, in and into darkness. God's go up, out and into light. Job pleads that the day of his birth would perish, its morning stars become dark and no shout of joy be heard (3:3–9); God celebrates creation's birth, when 'the morning stars sang together and all the angels shouted for joy' (38:7). God commends the sea's eruption from its womb; Job wills that the womb he left were locked. Job zooms in on one man (himself), one time (the day of his birth) and one circumstance (his present suffering); God zooms across creation's vast array, from expansive constellations to fragile ostrich eggs, from storehouses of snow to desolate deserts, from lightning strikes to raven's chicks. Job curses his existence; God glories in the majesty of creation and the beauty of life. God's vision is limitless; Job's is constrained.

I imagine that many of us, like Job, look down and in when we are going through difficult times. Alter's analysis brings into sharp focus the book of Job's call to, instead, look up and out.

4 The suffering king

2 Samuel 15:1–14; Matthew 26:36–55

Richard Hays' *Echoes of Scripture in the Letters of Paul* (Yale University Press, 1989) has prompted renewed interest in New Testament allusions to Old Testament passages. What counts as an allusion is debated and not easily defined, partly because context is key. If I say, 'I have a dream that poverty is no more,' I am alluding to Martin Luther King's famous speech. If I say, 'I have a dream to travel the world,' although certain words are the same, there is no allusion. Disagreements as to what is and is not an Old Testament allusion therefore arise. Nevertheless, attention to Old Testament resonance has born much fruit.

One recent example is the connection Nathan Johnson sees between Matthew's passion narrative and David's flight from Absalom ('The Passion according to David', *CBQ* 80, no. 2, 2018: 247–72). Johnson notes that 'the Mount of Olives' appears just twice in the Old Testament. One of these occurrences is in 2 Samuel 15:30, where David is described weeping as he flees from his son. This is significant, given the connection in Matthew's gospel between the Mount of Olives and Jesus' anguish. Similarly, Johnson argues, the weariness of Jesus' disciples mirrors the exhaustion of David's followers (Matthew 26:40–45; 2 Samuel 16:2, 14; 17:2). Jesus' exhortation 'Rise! Let us go' brings to mind David's 'Get up! Let us flee' (2 Samuel 15:14, NRSV). Judas' kiss to metaphorically stab Jesus in the back brings to mind Joab's kiss and literal stabbing of Amasa (2 Samuel 20:8–10). Jesus' instructions to Peter to withdraw his sword evoke David's command to Abishai to do likewise (2 Samuel 16:9–10).

Alluding to this tragic event in David's life when describing the most painful period in Jesus' life accords with Matthew's consistent portrayal of Jesus as the Davidic king. However, Jesus is not simply another David; he surpasses David. Regarding parallels that Johnson sees between Judah's betrayal of Jesus and Ahithophel's betrayal of David (2 Samuel 17:1–2, 23), he observes that, whereas Ahithophel's plans would have taken David by surprise, Jesus foresees and announces Judas' arrival before he comes. Significantly, although most Davidic references in Jewish literature focused on David's strengths and military expertise, it is David's weakness and suffering that is invoked here. Jesus is not the militant David, smiting his foes on every side, but the David who suffers, rather than retaliates, trusting his Father for the throne that is his.

5 Identifying 'I'

I attended a conference celebrating Richard Burridge's receipt of the 2013 Ratzinger Prize. The first presenter opened, 'We are here to celebrate Richard Burridge's prestigious award for arguing that the gospels are about Jesus.' The audience laughed. The gospels are obviously about Jesus. What Burridge had proved, however, is that the gospels fit into the genre of biography; their aim is to communicate the story of Jesus. This is in contrast to the belief, popular in the 20th century, that the gospels were directed at particular churches and aimed to address problems in those churches. Similarly, I remember a PhD student telling me that he aimed to prove that, when Paul writes 'I' in Romans 7, he is talking about himself. This too seems self-evident, but, like the intent of the gospels, has become much disputed.

The increasing interest in rhetorical criticism has contributed to the debate on Paul's 'I'. Ben Witherington III believes that Paul uses a rhetorical device called prosopopoeia. This involves playing the role of another (impersonation) for rhetorical effect. In Romans 7, Witherington argues, Paul plays the role of Adam, who enters Paul's argument in Romans 5:12–19. Paul invokes Adam not just as an individual but, as in Romans 5, an encompassing figure whose fallen condition is shared by all humanity (*Paul's Letter to the Romans*, Grand Rapids, 2004, pp. 179–205).

As Will Timmins notes, however, while Paul does invoke Adam, he is not 'playing the role' of Adam. Rather he is speaking of himself ('I') as one who is typical of Adam (*Romans 7 and Christian Identity*, CUP, 2017, p. 202). Why, then, does Paul write in the present tense of this sinful and ensnared existence (7:14–24)? Does this not contradict his celebration of the present liberation he experiences in Christ (7:25—8:17)? Putting these pictures side by side is not contradictory. Paul elsewhere speaks of the present reality of believers' transformed existence in Christ whilst also stressing the importance of the ongoing transformation that the Spirit brings. Believers have been freed by the new Adam (Christ) but they still need to put off the old.

6 Divine comedy?

Michelle V. Lee notes that apocalyptic literature 'involves not only the presentation of information, but the active involvement of the audience' ('A call to martyrdom,' *NovT* 40, no. 2, 1998: 164–94). It immerses people in an alternative view of reality so they can make right choices. Revelation draws the reader into God's perspective on the world, revealing how the lamb's victory brings God's kingdom to earth and what the believers' role in this is. It does so with dramatic effect, as the increased emphasis on literary criticism has highlighted. This emphasis has prompted an examination of Revelation in terms of narrative plot. Such analysis takes seriously the power of drama and narrative to affect change in people's perceptions, motivations and behaviour.

One noteworthy example is James Resseguie's contention that Revelation displays the U-shape of a classical comedy (*The Revelation of John: A narrative commentary*, Baker Academic, 2009, pp. 44–47). As the start of Revelation highlights, God and the lamb are sovereign and victorious; nothing can thwart their plans. Nevertheless, the narrative then descends as evil in its various guises stands against God's plans, with the dragon waging war against the woman's offspring and the beasts seeking to deceive the inhabitants of the earth into following them, not the lamb. The victory of the lamb is still assured, however, and, by the end of Revelation (chapters 21—22), all that is against God has received God's judgement and the bright glory of the new heavens and new earth is so perfect and secure that nothing vile or impure can enter it (21:27).

Comedy is perhaps not quite the right word to describe Revelation, given that, in common parlance, comedy depicts that which evokes laughter. Nevertheless, viewing Revelation as a U-shaped drama does fit the flow of the narrative. Moreover, it emphasises both the certainty of the lamb's victory and the reality of the difficulties that believers face as they seek to overcome the deceit of the beast and stay faithful to Jesus.

Guidelines

Focusing on the literary features of the biblical text does not undermine its historical reliability. When recounting events in our own lives, we pick our words carefully, thinking through what to include, what to exclude and how best to tell the story. Under the inspiration of the Holy Spirit, the biblical authors do this with great skill. The Bible contains much 'artful use of language', to borrow Robert Alter's phrase. The biblical authors' use of language emphasises, consolidates and enhances their message. Careful attention to the text therefore bears fruit, as the examples I have given this week demonstrate.

My hope in sharing these examples is to encourage you to pay close attention to the biblical text. Why has an author included some details but not others? What is the purpose of repeating certain things? Why have they used this particular imagery? Why have they structured their account in the way that they have? In particular, I encourage you to pay attention to a text's genre. A letter is written in a very different way than a story. A poem is different in style from a command. A proverb is not the same as a law. Awareness of the genre of a passage is vital for reading the text well.

However, careful attention to the artistry of a text is not just important because it illuminates the text's meaning, although it does. It also highlights the skill of the artist. In Genesis 1—2 we read of God's creation of a beautiful, vibrant and life-filled world. It is fitting, therefore, that the Spirit-inspired words we read in scripture are similarly beautiful, vibrant and life-filled. When we examine the intricacy and wonder of God's physical creation, we see something of the beauty and majesty of its creator. The Bible is an incredible piece of literature and, when we examine its intricacy and beauty, we see something of the wonder and majesty of the God who inspired it. Therefore, my hope is that attention to the detail of the text will not just illuminate your understanding of the Bible, but will also stir your heart to greater depths of praise and worship.

FURTHER READING

Robert Alter, *The Art of Biblical Narrative*, revised edition (Basic Books, 2011).

Robert Alter, *The Art of Biblical Poetry* (Basic Books, 2011).

Richard B. Hays, *Reading Backwards: Figural Christology and the fourfold gospel witness* (SPCK, 2015).

Stanley E. Porter and Bryan R. Dyer (eds), *Paul and Ancient Rhetoric: Theory and practice in the Hellenistic context* (CUP, 2016).

The letters of John

Terry Griffith

These three letters labour under a particular disadvantage: they come near the end of the New Testament. Almost certainly readers will already be familiar with John's gospel before discovering John's letters. Inevitably we will bring assumptions based on a prior knowledge of his gospel. This isn't necessarily a bad thing, as the two sets of documents are clearly related, but the independent contribution of the letters can be diminished simply because of this fact.

It is often assumed that the order in which they appear in the New Testament is the order in which they were written. If so, then we might view the letters as having been written to correct certain misinterpretations of the gospel. However, what if the letters are contemporaneous with or even prior to the gospel? How might this change our *appropriation* of their message?

Furthermore, if we think that the gospel was written late, that would place the letters right at the end of the first century. This has led many interpreters to read the letters as a polemical response to early forms of second-century heresies known to us as Docetism and Gnosticism. But how might viewing these letters primarily through a pastoral lens change our *appreciation* of their message?

Such assumptions tend to produce highly complex interpretations of both the gospel and letters of John and their relationship to one another. But in many ways the letters are remarkably imprecise. There may well be simpler approaches that yield a better *apprehension* of what is 'going on'. This is what these notes attempt to do.

The challenge is to read these scriptures with fresh eyes and to rediscover profundity in John's apparent simplicity.

Unless otherwise stated, Bible quotations are taken from the TNIV.

1 Life and light

1 John 1:1—2:2

John starts in the way he means to continue, with a form of thought that circles round and revisits ideas and topics but with different angles of approach and emphases. His language is typically simple but not always precise and clear. However, it would be a mistake to assume that John is not a profound thinker.

The beginning of 1 John (1:1–5) echoes the beginning of John's gospel, which starts with creation and shares the concepts of the Word, of life and of light. However, the actions described have a particular association with the resurrection appearances of Jesus at the end of the gospels. John may not simply have in view the incarnation of Jesus but also his bodily resurrection: that is, not just creation but also new creation; not just life but also eternal life.

John uses the language of experience to confirm his message. But, as a pastor, he also wants to address the experience of the Christian life and speaks of joy, fellowship, sin and forgiveness in the opening verses. These themes are explored within a dualistic framework which seems rigid and simplistic to us. But, if there are many shades of grey, John reminds us that they only receive their definition from the duality of black and white.

However, John is a more subtle thinker than first appears. The circle of fellowship may be defined by walking within the light (1:7), but fellowship with God and with one another can only be maintained if we are prepared to live under the shadow of the cross (1:7; 2:2). We find in Christian experience that light and darkness do coexist. To deny this is to live a lie (1:8), to make God out to be a liar (1:10) and to deprive Jesus of his paramount role (2:1–2).

In John's gospel the role of 'advocate' is taken by the Holy Spirit, but here it is 'Jesus Christ, the Righteous One' (2:1). In Roman jurisprudence, the advocate is not a legal representative but someone whose status and mere presence beside the accused is sufficient to secure their vindication. Thus the blood of Jesus, God's Son (1:7), not only purifies us from the guilt and shame of sin but also secures our standing with a faithful and just God (1:9). The experience of fellowship with the Father and with one another depends on this Jesus.

2 Obedience and love

John returns to the theme of living in the light (vv. 9–10) but links it to the new theme of obedience (v. 3). The specific command to which John refers (vv. 7–8) must be the new command that Jesus gives his disciples: 'A new command I give you: love one another. As I have loved you, so you must love one another' (John 13:34). John is showing that in order to live in the light and to have fellowship with God, we must have fellowship with other believers. The circle of light is described around obedience to this central command. To disobey on this point is to leave truth behind, to enter falsehood (v. 4) and to go into darkness (v. 11). It is simple to understand, but how difficult to do!

John will return to the theme of God's love (v. 5) in a big way. Whether it is God's love for us or our love for God need not detain us here. The point is that without love for one another, we cannot say that we know God (v. 3), nor can we say that we are living as Jesus did (v. 6).

John plays with the idea of the 'newness' of the command, which is also an 'old' one because it belongs at the very foundation of the Christian community. Obedience to this command demonstrates that a new era has already begun, because the darkness is passing and the true light is beginning to shine. If Jesus is the 'light of the world' (John 8:12), then to walk as Jesus did is to continue to shine his light upon the world.

The duality of light and darkness is a universal concept, but John applies it in very practical and demonstrable terms (vv. 10–11). Imagine you are in a room which is totally dark. You cannot see to move around freely. You stumble and trip, because you cannot see where you are going. You are afraid of what else might be in the darkness. But when the light is switched on, everything is transformed!

Obedience to this new command brings a new freedom and heralds the new day, but only if it is practised in community. It was taught to them from the very start, but it has to be practised anew as each day dawns.

3 Family and the world

John pauses in this passage to provide context before specifically mentioning the threat posed by 'antichrists' (2:18). Verses 12–14 have an artificial structure serving to highlight the familial nature of Christian identity. This identity is formed against the backdrop of 'sin' (v. 12), 'the evil one' (vv. 13–14) and 'the world' (v. 15). More positively, however, this letter is replete with tender vocatives that strengthen identity as family in community.

We have already met one of them, 'dear friends' (2:7; literally 'beloved'). This affectionate form of address speaks to a fundamental equality in Christ. While John can distinguish between the 'we' and the 'you' (as in 1:3) when emphasising a certain authority, he is equally at home addressing believers as 'brothers and sisters' (3:13). Indeed this is the most common term which John uses in this letter to describe Christians.

However, John's most common form of address is 'dear children' (2:1, 12, 14, 18; 3:7, 18; 4:4; 5:21). Jesus also uses this way of speaking (John 13:33), which highlights his disciples' identity as children of God. There is also an implied authority in such a relationship. The use of 'fathers' and 'young men', however, is thematic. The one implies age or standing (as those who are 'from the beginning'). The other implies military age and strength (as those who 'overcome the evil one'). John evidently uses these terms of all believers.

It is unfashionable to speak of boundaries, as if these are necessarily obstacles that cause people to stumble. And yet the scripture that talks most about love also says, 'Do not love the world or anything in the world' (v. 15). The world is here portrayed extremely negatively under three aspects: lustful sensuality, selfish ambitions and self-indulgent pride (v. 16). Two reasons are given for John's prohibition: you cannot claim to love God and also love these things (v. 15); and these things are ephemeral (v. 17). To love God is to love to do his will and thus to inherit eternal life.

We are called to live in the world but not to be of the world. How to get this balance right is the fresh and difficult task of every generation in the church.

4 The antichrist and the anointing

1 John 2:18–27

1 John 2 provides a fellowship test (2:3–11), a moral test (2:15–17) and now a doctrinal test. Something crucial has recently happened that invokes the image of 'the last hour' and causes John to coin a new term: 'antichrist' (v. 18). There has evidently been some kind of calamitous disruption in the Christian community that has shaken them to the core (v. 19). In response, John highlights three things.

First, the importance of the fellowship (v. 19). This has already been addressed from the viewpoint of life within the community. But John struggles to account for those who were once a part of the community but are so no longer. A strong sense of betrayal is being conveyed here, but there is much more going on than a sense of personal hurt or disappointment that warrants the denunciatory description 'antichrists'. Something very significant has been broken.

Second, the importance of the truth (vv. 20–25). Those who have departed have lost something that is vital for their spiritual well-being. They have denied the Son and by so doing have also denied the Father, who has given his witness to his Son (vv. 22–23; 5:10). What they heard at the beginning is the fundamental issue, and it is this 'truth' that those who remain need to retain. In line with the gospel's own statement of purpose, it makes good sense to understand that what has been denied is the confession that Jesus is the Messiah, the Son of God (John 20:31; 1 John 4:15; 5:1, 5). The attractions of Judaism for Christians of Jewish descent remained strong, as the rest of the New Testament attests. Just as the Jewishness of John's gospel is now much better understood, so reading the letters against that same context may help us to understand them better.

Last, the importance of the Spirit (vv. 20, 26–27). The anointing is probably best understood as a reference to the Spirit of God (3:24; 4:6, 13). John writes to confirm them in their confession and experience of Jesus, which are precisely what has set them apart from their contemporaries. He reminds them that they are taught by the Spirit of God (John 6:45; 14:26). By focusing on their foundational confession of faith, John strengthens their sense of community identity and helps insure against further losses.

5 Righteousness and sin

The alarming mention of the last hour and the antichrist (2:18) now gives way to positive statements about the coming of Christ, the Christian hope and what it means and will mean to be children of God (2:28—3.3). For the first time, the concept of birth is used (2:29), and this becomes a significant part of John's pastoral toolkit. John needs to show how the children of God and the children of the devil are to be distinguished (3:10). While origins are important in John's thinking, his dualism on this point is asymmetric. He never refers to any as 'born of the devil'. People are described as 'children of the devil' because their choices and behaviour reveal them to be so.

Much pastoral confusion and disquiet has arisen from John's treatment of sin and lawlessness here. The wider eschatological context (2:18—4:3) is important for interpretation, plus the fact that his treatment of righteousness is narrowly defined. Thus, the one who 'does what is right' is described in terms of loving one's brothers and sisters (2:29; 3:10).

In eschatological contexts, the word 'lawlessness' takes on the nuance of end-time 'rebellion' in Jewish thought. The specific statements on sin in 3:6 and 3:9 do not then contradict those made earlier which refer to sin that *mars* fellowship with God and one another (similarly the formulaic 2:12 and 3:5). If sin here refers to rebellion, characteristic of the complete rejection of God's purpose at the end time, then such sin *destroys* fellowship with God and with believers. 3:9 may then be understood as: 'No one who has been born of God commits ultimate rebellion, because God's offspring [seed] remains in him; they cannot commit this sin, because they have been born of God' (my paraphrase).

The work of the devil from the beginning has been set on rebellion against God's plan. To reject the work of Christ is to reject all hope of forgiveness, which he alone provides (3:8). This is tough stuff, but it provides the distinguishing test and ups the value we need to place on fellowship with other believers (3:10).

6 Cain and Christ

1 John 3:11–24

John's only reference to an Old Testament character serves as an illustration of what he has just said. He has not been talking about 'continuing' to sin (3:6, 9), as found in many translations, but something much more specific, akin to Cain's hatred and murder of his own brother. The distinguishing feature between the children of God and those of the devil, from John's perspective, is whether we love or hate fellow-believers (3:10–12). Are we among those who will take their brother's life, or are we among those who will lay down their life for their brother? In this way, we know whether we stand on the side of life or of death (vv. 14–15).

The positive example of Jesus, however, shows us what true love looks like. Words or feelings of love remain theoretical until expressed in actual deeds (vv. 16–18). The sentimentalising of love, as in lyrics to the Beatles song 'All you need is love', falls far short of the sacrificial love of Jesus that Christians seek to emulate. John illustrates what it might mean to lay down our lives for one another by being willing to share our possessions with those who are in need.

It is interesting to see how the practical and the spiritual flow into one another in John's thought. This is not a duality that John accepts (but it is all too common in the church today). He moves seamlessly between material possessions, the condition of our heart before God, confidence before God in prayer, faith in Jesus, loving one another and receiving the Spirit of God (vv. 17–24). In fact, to a remarkable extent John places our experience of assurance with God within the orbit of the practical and sacrificial loving of our brothers and sisters in Christ.

The content of the 'command' requiring our obedience is most fully given here (v. 23). Actually, it is a dual command in the manner of Jesus' answer to the lawyer's question about which is the greatest commandment (Mark 12:30–31). However, the differences are striking. The focus is on belief in God's Son (and not on loving God) and loving fellow Christians (and not one's neighbours). These are the two main pastoral concerns of John's letter.

Guidelines

- How might the theme of 'walking in the light' (1:7) be used and abused in the context of church life? Is it necessary to be absolutely transparent with others in order to walk in the light? And yet, in the context of recovery ministries, honesty is essential when confronting problems of addiction, etc. What might be learned from such groups?

- What does it mean to walk as Jesus walked (2:6)? (Although the pronoun 'he' is unspecified, it makes by far the best sense here that Jesus is the referent.) Examine yourself with reference to Jesus' character, priorities and purposefulness.

- Inclusion is currently the name of the game in town. John's dualistic form of thought tends to heighten differences and strengthen boundaries. Christians have tended to be known for what we are against, but how much does what we are for actually require us to maintain our distinctiveness? How might the pursuit of 'relevance' in the church lead to compromise with the world (2:15)?

- We probably all know people whom we thought were strong Christians but who have given up their confession of faith (2:19). What were the factors that led them to this outcome? Do you still pray for them and keep contact with them? What helps you to maintain your confession?

- John's outlook has been described as 'sectarian' because of his dualism (3:10). This is an anachronistic and loaded term. Can we do away with boundaries and distinguishing marks and remain true to our Christian calling and history? What are our identity markers? How might our brothers and sisters in the suffering church read this letter and how might they challenge us?

- How comfortable do you feel that John does not seem to address the need to love one's neighbour as oneself? How much influence does Jesus' command to his disciples, that we should love one another *as he has loved us*, have on your relationships with other Christians (3:16)? Think of a Christian you love least of all. Is this a true and accurate measure of your love for God, according to John?

1 False prophets and the Spirit of truth

1 John 4:1–6

John introduces the Spirit at the end of chapter 3 and now develops the theme along confessional lines (see also 1 Corinthians 12:3). The right confession of Jesus is part of our obedience. The 'Spirit of truth and the spirit of falsehood' (v. 6) distinguishes between those whom John calls 'friends' and 'false prophets' (v. 1). The Spirit of God is self-evidently opposed to the spirit of the antichrist (vv. 2–3). This is perhaps the most dualistic passage in 1 John and produces a hard line between the 'world' and 'us' (vv. 4–5). We can compare the language and conceptual framework of this passage with John 15:18—16:4, in which 'the world' is clearly aligned with Jewish opposition (see also John 18:20).

Jesus caused division during his ministry, and John Stott captured this well in his book entitled *Christ the Controversialist* (Tyndale Press, 1970). Those who were not with Jesus were against him (Matthew 12:30). His followers cannot avoid this difficult reality either, as they seek to proclaim Christ. The question is: which Christ? What are John's readers required to test as they examine what is said about Jesus?

The phrase 'Christ has come in the flesh' (v. 2) can be satisfactorily explained as expressing the *fact* of Jesus' incarnation rather than the *mode* of his incarnation. It is not difficult to find texts where the phrase 'to come in the flesh' is parallel to the phrase 'to enter the world'. Indeed, this same parallel essentially appears with reference to the antichrist (v. 3). We can also compare other Johannine statements of faith, such as 'the Son of God has come' (5:20) and especially Martha's 'I believe that you are the Messiah, the Son of God, who was to come into the world' (John 11:27).

All interpretations of Jesus inevitably reflect to a greater or lesser extent the cultural values of their respective contexts and, accordingly, may distort his image. However, a most significant advance in recent scholarship has been the recovery of the Jewishness of Jesus. It is *this* Jesus, as Messiah, who is to be confessed (v. 3) and to whom the Spirit of truth always leads (v. 6). Issues of truth and falsehood cannot be avoided when it comes to confessing Jesus.

2 Love and sacrifice

The danger in this section is to hold statements like 'let us love one another' (v. 7) and 'God is love' (vv. 8, 16) in isolation from each other. There is a specific content and shape to Christian love. It is not of love in general that John speaks, but of a particular love, otherwise 'everyone who loves has been born of God and knows God' (v. 7) would apply equally to the atheist.

Our responsibility to love our neighbours *as ourselves* is not in question. It is the responsibility to love our brothers and sisters in Christ *as he has loved us* that is in view here (vv. 20–21). This kind of love is the reflex to the love that has already been shown to us by God (vv. 11, 19). It also has a sacrificial inspiration and shape to it. It is defined by his sending his Son into the world so that we might live through him (v. 9). More specifically, God's love is expressed by the sending of his Son as an atoning sacrifice for our sins (v. 10). It has a clear salvific purpose. Astonishingly, Timothy Rees' (1874–1939) hymn 'God is love' (based on v. 8) omits any mention of the atoning death of Christ on the cross. He wills the end without indicating the means, and this simply does not do justice to John's teaching on God's love. The particularity of the incarnation continues to cause scandal, as it always has done.

Such a love is absolutely grounded precisely because it is sacrificial. Popular notions of love are all too often focused on the sentimental and the sexual, or on notions of individual freedom. Sacrificial love, however, is focused on laying down one's life (3:16) and the holiness of God. If we are tempted to give up this way of life as it's too hard, we are urged to remember God's love (v. 16).

Loving the Christian community is difficult but rewarding. John seems to be saying that God's indwelling of us is linked in some way to loving one another (v. 12). It is not only the matter of rightly confessing God's Son by the Spirit that brings us into close fellowship with the Father (vv. 14–15). The security of our relationship with God, both now and in the future, is also bound up with the way we love (vv. 16–18). This is how we know God (v. 20).

3 Victory and testimony

Love is not a matter of mere feeling but of obedience to God's commands. The evidence that believers are born of God is not just a true confession of faith about Jesus (vv. 1, 5), nor is it just a love for God as Father, but it is the love we have for all those who call God their Father – our sisters and brothers in Christ (4:21—5:2). Such a requirement is not burdensome (v. 3). In the words of Bobby Scott and Bob Russell, 'He ain't heavy, he's my brother.'

Victory is a theme that John has used before in relation to overcoming the evil one (2:13–14) and the false prophets (4:4). Such victory is won by the indwelling word of God (2:14) and the indwelling Spirit of God (4:4). Here, the victory is achieved by the confession of Jesus as the Son of God (v. 5). In that case, it is not only our faith as a personal quality that is in view but also the faith that is confessed (John 20:31).

The next verses (vv. 6–12) have occasioned much debate, but the discussion must not be divorced from the theme of testimony. There are three sources of testimony that God has given concerning his Son – the Spirit, the water and the blood (vv. 7–8). If we ask what it was that made Johannine Christianity distinctive within its Jewish milieu, then we will not go far wrong in trying to make sense of John's somewhat enigmatic statements. The experience of the Spirit of truth is vouchsafed to them (as it was also to Jesus) and enables witness to Jesus. The water evokes Jesus' own baptism and the rite of baptism that provides entrance into the church. The blood recalls the death of Christ for the forgiveness of sins and which sustains the church through regular worship centred upon the Lord's Supper.

These three activities together produce a combined testimony which defines the life and witness of any church community. They keep us focused on the Son of God, who is the source of eternal life (v. 11). The choice concerning this Jesus could not be more stark (v. 12). The veracity of God's testimony is at stake (v. 10).

4 Prayer and confidence

This closing section picks up many of the themes of the letter with the aim of bolstering confidence and assurance on the basis of what believers 'know' (vv. 13, 15, 18–20). John returns to a dualistic framework of thought to bolster their sense of identity as a community (vv. 18–21).

John's approach to God is full of confidence or boldness in this letter. For the confident believer there is no shame (2:28), no condemnation (3:19–22), no fear (4:17–18) and no doubt (vv. 14–15). Taken on their own, verses 14–15 set up the problem of finding out what God's will is. Perhaps it is better to interpret these general comments with reference to the particular issue of prayer concerning sin (not) leading to death (vv. 16–17).

Tertullian, in the second century, understood the distinction between life and death here as based on John's earlier teaching on sin (dealt with in two parts in 1:5—2:2 and 3:4–10). The former relates to sin that *breaks* fellowship and which can be forgiven and results in the restoration or renewal of life. The latter relates to sin that *destroys* fellowship and which cannot be forgiven because the only source of forgiveness has been utterly rejected. The end of this course of action is death. Thus John's twofold categorisation of sin (vv. 16–17) lends itself well to the interpretation of 3:9 (those born of God do not sin) as referring specifically to the sin that leads to death (v. 18).

We may have confidence in prayer that God will restore believers to 'life'. However, no such confidence exists for those who have abandoned the faith. Interestingly, John does not specifically say that they should not pray about that, but only 'I am *not saying* that you should pray about that' (v. 16). There is a subtle difference.

We have returned to the opening themes of living both in the light and under the shadow of the cross (1:7). This is the only safe place to be for the Christian. The best way to deal with any fear of apostasy is by daily committing oneself to live in, and return to, the grace and love of God so freely and fully portrayed at the cross of Christ. Those who do so may enjoy the confidence spoken of in this passage without falling into the sins of arrogance or presumption.

5 Love and truth

Strictly speaking, the letters of John are anonymous. The writer of this and the following postcard-length letter simply styles himself as 'the elder', which is a term of seniority and authority. Its unique use, without an accompanying name, shows that he is well-known. There are many theories about the identity of the author(s), but we simply do not know if it was John the apostle, the beloved disciple (if different) or John the elder (if different from the beloved disciple, and known from an early Christian source). Similarly, the addressee is unknown. Is the lady a woman who leads a church in her house, or is it code for a church (the bride of Christ)?

John's core values are love and truth, which appear like conjoined twins (vv. 1–6; Ephesians 4:15). Truth is said to indwell us and to be enduring (v. 2), and it ushers in a certain way of life characterised by love (vv. 4, 6). Love and truth are closely connected with grace, mercy (only found here in the gospel and letters) and peace (v. 3), and produce joy (v. 4).

The truth has its focus on Jesus as the Messiah who has really come (v. 7). This is what the deceivers and the antichrists have denied by their going out into the world. Those who go forth in this way have not remained in the teaching of/about the Messiah, unlike those who have remained, who have both the Father and the Son (v. 9).

Love does not require these believers to further the work of those who actively oppose Johannine teaching (vv. 10–11). Those who travelled between scattered Christian communities were dependent upon household hospitality (3 John 5–8). These household churches, built on truth, were the result of what had been worked for and are the evidence for the reward due (v. 8; see 1 Corinthians 3:10–15). But there is also a wicked work in which they should play no part. The particularity of truth, which for the Christian is Jesus-shaped, has capacity for diversity within it, but love should not be used as a pretext to mask real differences.

6 The Name and the names

With no direct references to 'Jesus' or 'Lord', this letter is unique in the New Testament. Other unusual features of 3 John are the very Jewish reference to 'the Name' (this can only be the name of Jesus in this context), the Jewish perspective of the reference to 'the pagans' (v. 7) and the use of 'the friends' as a descriptor of the Christian community (v. 14; John 15:14–15). While short, this personal letter reveals a lot that is going on through the mention of various characters, although the detail is very thin.

The elder acts as a pastor should. The phrase 'I love' is found only five times in the New Testament, and this is one of them (v. 1). He shows his care for Gaius' well-being in a conventional blessing (v. 2). He expresses joy in his faithfulness (v. 4), offering encouragement in what he is doing (vv. 5, 8) as well as instruction (v. 11).

Gaius was faithful to and walked in the truth and is presumably a church leader (v. 3). He is hospitable to Christians unknown to him and is supportive of their ministry and mission (vv. 5–6). The brothers and sisters are probably missionaries to the Gentiles. Although unnamed, it was probably enough for them that they should be simply referred to as those who worked for the sake of 'the Name' (v. 7; Acts 5:41).

Diotrephes, however, is ambitious and is a malicious gossip with scant regard for truth. Furthermore, with his policy of not welcoming others, he brooks no disagreement and acts in an authoritarian way over his church (vv. 9–10). Here is clear evidence that churches in the early years had to deal with those who regarded themselves as unaccountable to anyone.

Demetrius is likely the person bearing the letter and comes with a glowing recommendation (v. 12). He is not only spoken well of by everyone and by the elder, but even 'the truth itself' speaks well of him. Only a few of the names of the countless early Christian witnesses have been preserved. The desire to be first, and thus recognised and known, is an insidious temptation. Diotrephes has become infamous for this reason and would make a good patron saint of the personality cult. While it is right that we should honour others appropriately, we should always remember that it is never about 'me' or 'you'. What are our names compared with the Name?

Guidelines

- The gospel has been tragically perverted and misused in Christian tradition to justify anti-Semitism. Do you think the language in the Johannine literature is anti-Semitic and, if so, why (1 John 4:3; John 8:44)? What mitigations would you place on language used in the Johannine literature that might be construed as anti-Semitic, particularly when teaching and preaching?

- How does the fact that God/Christ loves us/the church (1 John 4:11) help you to love those who charitably might be called 'difficult' brothers and sisters in Christ? How do we come to terms with Christians who have opposed or hurt us in some way?

- How important is the 'givenness' of God's testimony about his Son (1 John 5:9)? Did those 21 Christians martyred on the beach in Libya by ISIL in 2015 waste their lives because they refused to give up this testimony? What about you?

- How do John's words challenge your approach to and experience of prayer (1 John 5:14–15)? Reflect on whether it is possible to avoid the Scylla of presumption and the Charybdis of doubt in prayer. Where does the Holy Spirit fit into your theology and practice of prayer?

- I have stood in front of Salvador Dalí's *Christ of St John of the Cross* in the Kelvingrove Art Gallery and Museum in Glasgow. In it is a blank titulus, no nails, no crown of thorns, no blood and a free-floating cross. We are invited to look down on Salvador Dalí's cosmic Christ and assume a divine viewpoint. How do you think John might assess this, perhaps most famous, portrayal of the crucifixion of Christ? Why do you think Dalí's painting is so popular?

- In what ways is hospitality different from entertaining? How can a ministry of hospitality, individually or corporately, be used as a spiritual discipline in the local church and extend the reach of Christian mission? How do you respond to the fact that both the Elder in 2 John and Diotrephes in 3 John exclude some people from their circle?

FURTHER READING

Karen H. Jobes, *1, 2, and 3 John* (Zondervan, 2014).

Spirituality and mission 20:20

Kate Bruce

What we see is deeply affected by what we expect to see. Recently, I got glasses. Trees in the distance are not blurry. Who knew? As my sight deteriorated, I had simply accepted blurry vision as the norm. Realising my 'blindness' was something of a shock. We see what we expect to see, but that doesn't mean we have clear vision.

How we see the world physically affects how we interact with it. The same is true in spiritual terms. There is a clear link between spirituality and mission. What takes shape in our words and actions is an expression of our internal world (Matthew 15:18). The way we act externally also affects who we are and who we are becoming. Our habits shape us. How, then, do we cultivate good spiritual habits, holy habits?

Picture a yacht on the sea. The helm is steering a compass bearing. If she takes her eye off the compass and fails to attend to the direction of the wind and tug of the tidal undercurrents, the boat will drift off course. There is something here about intention, attention and focus.

With that in mind, week 1 of these notes will explore an intentional spirituality marked by love, prayer, humility, trust, contemplation and joy. Week 2 will explore how this spirituality embraces mission as an expression of divine love, listening to God's Spirit and being honest, imaginative, pastorally attentive and confident.

Christian spirituality is a broad subject, as indeed is mission. These notes cannot hope to be exhaustive, but the aim is to stimulate reflection and stir us into action.

Unless otherwise stated, Bible quotations are taken from the NRSV.

1 Love: the foundation of all spirituality

Matthew 22:34–40; 1 Corinthians 13:1–8

Jesus shows us that love is foundational. First, love God with all your being. This involves the active intention to steer a certain course. Our love for God comes from the knowledge that he loved us first (1 John 4:19); his very nature is love (1 John 4:16b). We must begin here. If we try to earn God's love, we will spend our lives motoring along a highway of shoulds and oughts in the hope that clocking up enough miles will earn love. That's a lot of pointless travel, given that we are *already* loved.

From this foundation Jesus calls us to love others as we love ourselves. Many carry the wounds of rejection and profound hurt and wall off the more vulnerable parts of themselves, resistant to divine and human love. But to grow in love, we must allow ourselves to be loved, admitting to our need and vulnerability. This is a journey of learning to trust God and others. The enemies of this process are fear and pride, which can rugby-tackle us as we attempt to reach out. However, to establish a firm spiritual foundation, we must receive love and live from this basis. It doesn't matter a whit if the journey takes one step forwards and two back, as long as the intention is there.

Paul writes about an ongoing spiritual workout, an intentional desire to love and live out of love. He highlights the hallmarks of genuine love. It's hard not to wince as we recall our flawed attempts at love – the impatient explosions at the kids, unkind words about a colleague, the longing of the green-eyed monster, crude behaviour, self-promotion, hot-tempered out-bursts, ruminating from the place of fearful insecurity over perceived slights and so forth.

Perhaps the image of a training programme might help stave off despair. As part of my job I undertake periodic fitness tests. One aspect of the test is press-ups. When I began training, a couple of years ago, I couldn't execute a single press-up. I had no upper body strength. With my trainer I began a pro-gramme of weight training. With focus, time and effort, eventually I managed one press up, then two, and built on that. In the same way, in the spiritual gymnasium of our lives, what matters is the intent of the human heart: love.

2 Prayer: God awaits us

Romans 8:26–27; Matthew 6:5–13; 1 Thessalonians 5:17
Words from 1 Thessalonians spring to mind: 'Pray without ceasing.' My inner nine-year-old pipes up incredulously, 'Without ceasing? Are you mad? Impossible! The living only do one thing without ceasing: breathing.' Exactly. Prayer is the natural orientation of the heart, just as drawing breath is the natural disposition of the living. It's not that prayer is difficult; it's that we allow everything else to conspire to make it seem so. Prayer is the heart's true north. When we stop fighting and come to rest, we find the presence of God. When we stop striving, preening and fretting, and close the door of our inner room (actual or metaphorical), there is God – waiting, welcoming our stumbling attempts, drawing us into silence. In this quiet place we come before Abba, knowing and being known. All our gifts, wounds and scars are seen. God knows every desire of our hearts – the good, the bad and the ugly – and asks that we hand all to him in trust.

In the Lord's Prayer, Jesus gives us the shape and content of our prayers. Paul reminds us that God breathes his prayer in us. This is the heart's true north, if we would simply relax and trust. The needle of our intention flickers about as we resist this union. In fear, we flee from such prayer into the control room of our imagined self-shaped destiny. This concrete bunker is a lonely, futile place.

We are not left alone, struggling to shape a worthy prayer, hammering it out on the anvil of self-righteousness. Our spirituality grows out of openness to God praying in us, shaping our babbling, moulding it into his prayer for us and for the world.

If I said to you, 'Breathe without ceasing,' you'd look at me as though I were mad. 'I can't help breathing. I'm a natural at it,' you would reply. If we could grasp the simple wisdom of applying this to prayer, we would rediscover the contemplative trust of the child absorbed in the moment: trusting, drinking it all in, shaping and being shaped. If we would stop being so grown-up, proud and pompous, we might discover the truth: 'I can't help praying. I'm a natural at it.'

3 Humility: 'We have this treasure in clay jars'

2 Corinthians 4:7; Luke 18:9–14; Romans 7:14–25

Pride is a block to spirituality. When pride has us in its grip, we live in a hall of distorting mirrors in which our finer points are magnified until we cannot truly see ourselves; our frailties skulk in shadow, fearful of discovery.

Jesus tells the parable of the Pharisee and the tax-collector to those who are hostages in the house of pride. The tax-collector understands humility. He is made of clay, and he knows it. From his self-knowledge he cries for God's mercy. In contrast, the Pharisee is the boastful, self-made man. He acts as though God doesn't see him with 20/20 clarity; he is all spin and bluster – a peddler of fake news. We cannot present our best side to God and hope to airbrush the rest out. To even attempt this is profoundly counterproductive. God sees us as we are and meets us in this reality. To play the Pharisee card is the equivalent to going to the doctor with a major infection and claiming to be in tip-top health. Unless we acknowledge our sickness, how can we be healed? Notice that it is the tax-collector who goes home justified before God. The Pharisee leaves as he arrived: lost.

Humility before God breeds confidence in God. Look at Paul, who had every reason to feel he was 'the man'. However, he recognised that all his human standing paled to nothing before the 'surpassing value of knowing Christ Jesus my Lord' (Philippians 3:8). He writes in Romans of his human weakness, his inability to do the good he wants to do, the recognition of the power of sin at work in him. He speaks with honesty about this struggle and expresses confidence in Jesus who will rescue him.

Humility before others breeds compassion and forges connections. When I am honest about my failures, I make space for you to be honest about yours. We are not in competition, but are forging an alliance based on love.

Humility before God opens possibilities, while pride simply bolts the door. The humble heart says to God, 'Potter, throw me on the wheel again, for I cannot make myself.' The process of new creation begins. Here is hope.

4 Trust: 'Underneath are the everlasting arms'

Matthew 7:7–12; Isaiah 43:1–7

Picture a child on the edge of a pool, in which her parent stands ready to catch her. Look at how she hurls herself off the side, trusting the arms beneath to catch her. It's a deeply appealing image. Jesus paints a picture of God as one to be utterly trusted, the giver of good gifts. Isaiah speaks of God who rescues his people because they are precious, honoured and beloved daughters and sons. Fierce love seeks to elicit deep trust.

Sadly, many children and vulnerable adults have been offered the equivalent of stones by people whose duty was to provide care and nurture. How easily mistrust can corrode the human heart. One of the greatest spiritual challenges we face, as a result of the abuse scandal, is lack of trust in the church, which easily distorts trust in God. For those whose capacity to trust has been deeply damaged by abuse, the idea of such trust may be profoundly challenging. Mistrust locks people up in citadels, where the illusion of control brings a degree of comfort but limits the capacity to receive love, to see God at work and to allow this perception to deepen trust. Trust invites us to lower the drawbridges and allow God over the threshold. How do we do this? It is an act of trust to whisper anxieties and legitimate fears into the divine ear. Trust is still trust, however slowly it moves.

Frequently, God's reassurance to 'be not afraid' is followed by dynamic change and opportunity. Abraham, Moses, Joshua, Samuel, Elijah, Jeremiah, Ezekiel, the people of Israel – are all offered reassurance at moments of invitation to new possibility. This call to trust is most clear in Gabriel's words to Mary: 'Do not be afraid' (Luke 1:30). Trust opens doors to possibilities: the possibility of hope, healing and new life. This call to trust is not a pink, fluffy invitation to an easy life. Trust does not erase pain and struggle – just ask Mary! However, it is a call to deeper union with God and deeper connection with each other.

We may not identify with the child who hurls herself with abandon into the waiting arms. However, the willingness to approach those arms, however hesitantly, is an act of spiritual courage and strength. It doesn't matter how we reach God: one giant leap of faith or many small steps of trust. Either way, 'underneath are the everlasting arms' (Deuteronomy 33:27, NIV).

5 Contemplation: 'Consider the lilies'

Matthew 6:25–34; 13:31–32

To contemplate is to look beyond the obvious to what lies within. Often we rush, hurrying to ensure all bases are covered, all needs met, all targets hit. Jesus' words in Matthew 6 are a balm to the anxious soul. To consider the birds of the air and the lilies of the field, we first have to stop and notice. Half the time we are not looking, so we miss the wisdom God imparts. Sunlight catching a droplet of water on a blade of grass is infinitely more valuable than the most expensive diamond; you cannot own it, chisel it, shape and set it. It just is: beautiful, simple and there – pure gift. How many gifts do we fail to see because we are sleepwalking through life?

Jesus' teaching is often based on what he notices in the world around him and how this speaks of God. He does not despise the little and the local, seeing here the rich potential to teach deep spiritual truth. Contemplating the natural world leads him to encourage his friends not to worry. Then, as now, worry is carbon monoxide to the soul. Contemplation, seeing clearly, brings in fresh air.

Contemplation helps us to notice potential in the smallest of things. Jesus sees potential in a mustard seed to grow into something marvellous. How often do we write things off as too small, too insignificant, too little? The contemplative heart knows that smiling at a stranger can lift their heart, courtesy to another driver can avert a world of road rage and a gentle word can turn aside a torrent of abuse.

Contemplation slows us down in a world that is often rushing relentlessly; then we start to really notice. Such seeing is deeply sustaining. My late spiritual director once asked me, at a point when my mood was low and my faith wobbly, 'Why do you keep on going on this spiritual path?' I pondered for a while and the answer came to me, 'Because of green.' We sat in silence considering this rather odd answer. It came from my walk to work. Many times, I had noticed the variety of green in the canopy and undergrowth, more shades than I could count. Somehow, this noticing sustained me when life seemed drab, giving hope, faith and strength, reminding me of the infinite creativity of God.

6 Joy: 'May those who sow in tears reap with shouts of joy'

Psalm 126:5; Isaiah 61:1–4; Philippians 4:4–7

Joy is a word that could do with being freed from association with saccharine, trite sentiment. In a world where cynicism and bitterness often rule the day, the image of joy skipping along in pink satin, waving a cross-stitched motivational Bible verse is not going to cut it. In a context where the spectres of racism, abuse, violation, hunger and suffering stalk about with impunity, where the dividing line between real and fake news is presented as porous, a weak understanding of genuine joy is going to get bulldozed.

Genuine joy does not glitter-coat life's challenges and say, 'There, there, it's all alright.' Joy, rooted deep in the knowledge of the Lord, who saw beyond the suffering of the cross without denying its reality, is well able to gaze into despairing eyes with compassion. Such joy sits with the oppressed, the broken-hearted and the downtrodden and holds out hope. In gentleness, joy reframes the suffering against the greater backdrop of God's loving reality, offering comfort in this process. Joy can coexist with tears and grief, and has no need to whitewash pain and suffering. Joy receives the ashes of despair with great care, knowing that there will be a garland, but aware that in the waiting there is profound pain.

This is as much decision as emotion; it lies in the resolve to trust and hope in God's present loving kindness. Joy refuses to be squashed by the forces of despair or the agencies of cynicism and hatred. Joy is gutsy, faithful, determined and ultimately hopeful. When people are jaded and tired, when politics seems bewildering and mistrust is rife, the world needs people who are grounded and joyful.

Joy understands that death never has the last word. Joy laughs with delight at the case of mistaken identity in that garden in the early morning light. Joy is confident in the day when sorrow and sighing will flee away.

A spirituality marked by joy is full of hope, bathed in compassion, willing to sit in dark places, but always looking for the light. Joy is a repairer and a healer. 'May those who sow in tears reap with shouts of joy' (Psalm 126:5). Bring on the joy!

Guidelines

- I've offered six virtues: love, prayer, humility, trust, contemplation and joy. Limited to six, what spiritual attributes would you select and why?

- Jesus said, 'You shall love the Lord your God with all your heart, and with all your soul, and with all your mind' (Matthew 22:37). Ponder each word – 'heart', 'soul' and 'mind' – and ask what it means to love God with each part of yourself now, in the midst of your everyday life.

- Jesus also said, 'You shall love your neighbour as yourself' (Matthew 22:39). In what ways do you love yourself?

- Take five minutes today to stop and breathe – to recognise that God breathes prayer in and through you.

- Do you identify readily with the child who hurls herself into her parent's arms, or are you more hesitant? Talk to God about this.

- Take a walk, or sit in the open, and notice. Look at the plants, the varieties of colour. Listen to the sounds. Notice the insects. Pay attention to people around you. Notice without judgement. Be present to God in the moment. Behold and know you are being beheld.

- Whatever you face at the moment, what does the decision to be joyful mean? Remember joy is not a denial of pain, but the decision to acknowledge suffering and look beyond it in hope.

- Look back over the notes this week. Has anything been particularly helpful or unhelpful? Notice this and bring it to God.

1 Loving: 'For God so loved the world'

Genesis 1:27–31; John 3:16–21

How we understand mission is based on our image of God. What is God like? What does God desire? I often find myself wrestling with two divine images. One is of an angry, exacting God, frowning and perpetually cross – a divine bully boy. The other is unremittingly kind, caring and understanding, and a bit of a pushover – a divine fairy godmother. Neither are correct images. How about if we start with goodness, love and holiness as inherent characteristics of God and work from there?

God creates the world and it is good. Women and men are created in the image of God, fundamentally and originally good. Original goodness is so much more appealing than original sin. Hand in hand with this goodness is love. Jesus comes into the world not to condemn it, but to save it: 'For God so loved the world…' (John 3:16). What do we need saving from? From ourselves: from our propensity to do stupid, selfish and destructive things; from our failure to love and allow ourselves to be loved; from weaknesses that unchecked draw us into darkness. God is holy and no pushover. God's light exposes darkness and seeks to eradicate it, out of a desire to love and restore goodness. God pursues us with a holy love.

What does that mean for mission? How we are to be in the world? The starting point has to be love: genuine love for the people and environment around us, a willingness to recognise the potential for good, even in unlikely places, and the courage to call out evil for what it is.

Can we see the goodness in creation, naming the beauty of the opening rose? This is mission. Can we support and celebrate the goodness in communities that cooperate, in the hardworking MP, in the ethically minded business leader? This is mission. Can we love the angry child, see beyond the bitterness of the jilted lover to reach the hurting soul within? This is mission. We live in a time when untruth is peddled as reality and lies abound. Can we call out the distortions, name the evil and point to the one who died to save us from our ugly attitudes and behaviours? This is mission in the name of Jesus, who is good, loving and holy.

2 Listening: 'While Peter was still thinking about the vision, the Spirit said to him...'

Acts 10:9–23

The word 'mission', and its sidekick 'evangelism', have a tendency to press all my inadequacy buttons; I'm just not that good at it. I have encountered forms of mission that are so certain, so arrogant and so incapable of listening to the other that I cringe. I can't subscribe to a view of mission that requires me to push my version of God at a waiting world, on my terms, steamrollering all doubts. When I remember those wonderful words *missio Dei*, relief is palpable: it's God's mission. I don't have to be a paragon of missional certitude. I just have to be me, listening as best I can, open and willing. Engagement in mission naturally flows out of prayerful spirituality – and that simply requires the intention to attend to God.

We see in the book of Acts, again and again, that God's Spirit drives the church's outreach. The scope of that mission is well beyond anything the early church might have dreamt up in a committee meeting of good ideas. In Acts 10, we see the wonderfully outrageous scope of God's mission stretching out to embrace Gentiles.

Peter's vision and the events around it draw the attention of the fledgling church to the Gentile communities. Peter had turned aside, intending to pray, though his effort seems thwarted by the distraction of hunger. No matter, since God is able to use our intentions, however feeble. Three times God speaks to Peter through his hunger, and Peter is listening. In spite of the shocking message of the vision, directing Peter to ignore all he has learnt about purity, he doesn't push the vision away, dismissing it as a mere product of his hunger. He wonders about its meaning; he adopts a listening and open attitude and he hears God speak, instructing him to go with the men at the door. What follows is incredible. What might have remained a minor Jewish sect turns outwards to the whole world.

God's mission is always full of surprises. Are we listening? Are we willing to have our cultural and religious assumptions turned upside down? Are we willing to let God's plans unfold, or are we rather more concerned with our own bright ideas? God needs people who are available, whose intention is to listen, who are open to change. *Missio Dei*: it's God's mission, God's song. I'm starting to feel better already.

3 Honest: 'For I know my transgressions, and my sin is ever before me'

A friend of mine experienced the collapse of her marriage, resulting in divorce. They were a couple at the heart of their local church, doing all kinds of good works. Suddenly, she felt isolated and alone, a pariah. She received the message that good Christians are not supposed to experience imploding marriages. This attitude breeds hiddenness and dishonesty, peddling a superficial faith of the 'all's fine with me and the Lord' variety.

The person who knows themselves and trusts in God's love can afford to be honest. There is great freedom here. Expressed wisely, honesty creates connections, builds understanding and opens doors to healing and hope. There can be a disabling dishonesty in some forms of mission that imply that following the Christian path is straightforward, that there is no experience of or room for failure. However, when we are appropriately honest about our lives, genuine connections are forged and empathy can flourish. This builds communities of belonging.

In Psalm 51, David tells his truth, having failed spectacularly as a king, a husband and a man. Traditionally, it is accepted that the events of 2 Samuel 11—12 are behind this psalm. The great King David is reduced to a peeping tom, an adulterer, a liar and a murderer. In this psalm, David expresses radical honesty with God, without dissembling. He cries to God for cleansing, for a pure heart, for the continued presence of God's Spirit and for the restoration of joy. He is aware that he has committed evil and deserves none of these things, but he cries out anyway.

Then comes a fascinating move. From this cesspit of his own making, David says, 'Then I will teach transgressors your ways, and sinners will return to you' (v. 13). David is learning compassion, empathy and understanding. Who better to speak honestly of failure than the man who forged his own?

Sometimes it is easy to think that the mission of the church rests on the good people, the ones who have it all sorted – the shiny folks. I've listened to enough people over the years to realise that it isn't that straightforward. Often shiny happiness is a thin layer. It's those who know their mess and muddle, who have been found by God in their dark places, who can speak honestly and with empathy. Interesting that in David's honest lament, we see the seeds of missional intent.

4 Imaginative vision: 'How could we sing the Lord's song in a foreign land?'

Psalm 137; Ezekiel 37:1–14

'Where there is no vision, the people perish,' says Proverbs 29:18 (KJV). Without trust the vision never forms, and vision is essential to mission. The Christian vision looks to the transforming God, who overcomes death. Do I trust this God? If I do, then my eyes lift. I can reimagine the world in this light of hope. This is no candyfloss wishful thinking. The prophetic imagination sees things as they are, but also looks beyond the horizons of human failure into the vistas of divine possibility.

Ezekiel is caught up in a divine vision of a valley littered with bones: a picture of faithless Israel in exile, carted off to Babylon. Separated from Jerusalem and the temple, both of which will soon be utterly destroyed, they are far from all that is familiar and secure. It must seem that they are far from God. Ezekiel is literally and metaphorically preaching to the dead. How can they sing the Lord's song in this desperate place?

Ezekiel trusts God and receives the imaginative vision to see beyond despair. God includes him as his agent in this new work. Ezekiel prophesies, and transformation comes in a dance of fusion. He calls the *ruach* of God to come upon the bones, and they stand, a vast living, breathing multitude. From death valley a new thing is birthed.

The million-dollar question is always, 'And so what?' A spirituality which cultivates trust will have the willingness to confess, as well as the ability to reimagine. The mission of the church embraces speaking truth within the institution and offering new vision in the wider context. It takes trust in God to admit when we have got it wrong. Like Ezekiel staring at the horror of the bones, we must appreciate the appalling scale of the harm perpetrated by abuse in all its forms across denominations. There is no easy fix, no swift healing – but there is hope.

Imagine a church of transparency, safety and care, where vulnerability is honoured and protected and truth is told. Imagine safe spaces where sexual wounds are spoken of and appropriately tended. Imagine a church where people can trust, confess, express anger and find connection and healing – where differences are not ironed out, but honoured. A missional church will become this place. Wider culture needs to recognise these possibilities. Listen: with God, the bones are rattling!

5 Pastoral attentiveness: 'The angel... touched him, and said, "Get up and eat"'

1 Kings 19:3–9; Luke 8:40–56

In 1 Kings 19 we meet Elijah in a suicidal state. The ministering angel notices Elijah's need for affirmation and practical support, providing him with physical touch, food, water and the opportunity to sleep. There is no lecture about pulling himself together.

The healings in Luke 8 are full of examples of profound pastoral attentiveness. Jesus did not need to accompany Jairus to his house to heal is daughter; he had healed the centurion's servant from a distance (Luke 7:1–10). By walking with Jairus, Jesus is a supportive presence in a devastating situation.

When the haemorrhaging woman reaches out, hoping for healing but cloaked in the anonymity of shame, Jesus is attuned to her need for restoration. Twelve years of bleeding have left her ritually unclean, 'not good enough'. In asking who had touched him, Jesus creates a public scene that people will talk about; he will not allow her shame to keep her trapped. Her anonymity needs removing. Her healing needs public proclamation, so that she is free from the stigma placed on her by religious taboos. In naming her as 'daughter' he restores her, and in underlining her faith he praises her publicly such that finally she can find peace. Jesus deals with her with such sensitivity and care.

As he arrives at Jairus' house, the scene is chaotic. The word is that the little girl is dead. People are wailing. Jesus prevents too many people crowding into the house, protecting the bewildered and grieving parents. In the face of the certainty of her death, he declares, 'She is not dead but sleeping' (Luke 8:52). Practically, if they believe she is asleep, she is less likely to be treated as a curiosity in the community; no child needs this. In taking her by the hand, he breaks the taboos of death. In this touch, there is life. In instructing the parents to feed her, he restores them to the normality of providing for their child.

This attitude of careful attentiveness is critical to mission. How are people to ever believe God loves them if they are not treated with pastoral attentiveness? This is not a cloying, intrusive, smothering concern, but the quiet noticing and meeting of the other's needs. This is the sensitive attentiveness of the contemplative spirit.

6 Hopeful: 'You may know what is the hope to which he has called you'

Ephesians 1

The spiritual decision to be joyful – not in a frothy, frivolous way, but in a deeply grounded manner, choosing to look for God's loving kindness in all circumstances – cannot help but feed into a hopeful attitude.

Ephesians 1 is full of reasons to be hopeful for ourselves and our society. God blesses us, chooses us, adopts us, redeems us and forgives us – lavishing grace upon us. How many people struggle on in despair, abandoned, afraid and alone, not knowing that God desires them, and that they are inherently precious? How many people feel lost, crippled by guilt, unaware that God seeks them and forgives them? How many people feel that the world is in chaos and there seems to be no order, no plan and no direction? Many people are unaware that God holds creation in his hands – and has a purpose for all things, however broken they seem to us.

It's easy to lose hope when we cease to locate that hope in Christ. When hope wavers, mission initiatives look flimsy, knocked out by a committee of bright ideas. Hope in Christ grounds us. It reminds us that we have a message deeply relevant to our culture: an invitation into relationship with God, an invitation to become more fully who we are called to be. When human rule, authority, power and dominion rage and clash, we can have confidence in God's power which raised Christ from death and seated him far above all human agencies.

Now is the time for hearts to be enlightened and for a message of hope to sing out from Christian communities. That message needs earthing in practical ways; it is useless to speak theological truth without putting flesh on the words. It's no good assuring the lonely they are loved and never visiting them!

To allow cynicism, fear and despair to sound their discordant dirges unchallenged would be a colossal failure of mission. God invites the outsider, the broken, the grieving, the sinner and the saint to his table in a kingdom where there are no walls, no back rows, no second-class seats. This is the counternarrative to all intolerance, isolationism and downright nastiness spun by agencies of evil. Aware of our frailties, we may not have much confidence in ourselves as God's agents, but we can have tremendous hope in God.

Guidelines

- Consider the image of God you carry internally. Does it match with the image of God you present to the world or is there a clash between your inner thoughts and your external behaviours?

- What does 'mission and evangelism' mean to you? Do these words elicit any strong feelings, positive or negative? Bring this into your prayer.

- Are there things in your life that you feel make you somehow less 'good', less useful to God? Kintsukuroi is the Japanese art of mending cracks in pots with gold. As well as being beautiful, it serves as a reminder that our flaws and failings may have much to teach. Your cracks might be your greatest gifts in connecting to the world.

- Take time today to look at the things in the world that seem most broken, most beyond hope. Consider these things as bones in a dry valley. Allow your prayer to unfold, seeing life transform the place of death. Use your imagination to revision situations of hopelessness and offer that vision back to God.

- As you go about your day, slow down and notice the people around you – the woman struggling with the screaming toddler, the young people having a laugh, the schoolboy walking alone. Notice what you notice. Let your prayers go feral – and bring these people to God.

- Make the decision today to offer practical care and support to someone, to deliberately go out of your way to care.

- Make a list of all the reasons you have to hope in Christ. Write down ways in which you demonstrate that hope in your daily life.

- How can you engage in mission as the person you are, being natural, using all your gifts and flaws? Offer yourself to God again – in body, mind and spirit.

FURTHER READING

Nadia Bolz-Weber, *Accidental Saints: Finding God in all the wrong people* (Canterbury Press, 2015).

Judy Hirst, *A Kind of Sleepwalking: And waking up to life* (DLT, 2014).

Judy Hirst, *Struggling to be Holy* (DLT, 2006).

Anne Lamott, *Travelling Mercies: Some thoughts on faith* (Anchor Books, 1999).

Henri Nouwen, *The Inner Voice of Love: A journey through anguish to freedom* (DLT, 1997).

Peace revisited

David Kerrigan

The biblical notion of shalom, the Hebrew term for God's all-encompassing peace, was the subject of my 2018 Advent book published by BRF, *The Prince of Peace in a World of Wars*. Returning to the theme here gives me an opportunity to think afresh about the subject. One thing is unsurprising – nothing has lessened my sense that the peace of God is a gift sorely needed in our stressful times. But rather than offer a precis of parts of the book, I want to revisit some of the themes from a fresh angle. The first week will focus inwards to understand what we mean by the peace of God, and in the second week we will look at how we apply that in our daily lives.

My starting point will be the same, however: revisiting that final Passover evening, when Jesus shared a meal with his disciples. That night their fears came to the surface as they sensed all was not well. They were right, of course, for within hours Jesus would be arrested, and the day ahead would be worse than their greatest fears. Perhaps this is a note of realism with which to approach these two weeks of studies. Fears are often not illusions, but rather they are emotions that have their roots in circumstances that can't just be batted away or ignored. Likewise, the feelings that fear generates are real. It isn't a sign of weakness to admit to fear, to have qualms about an uncertain future, to long for a sense of calm when all around the storm is raging.

Here's the good news: this gift of peace is available to us. But it has to be understood aright – what it is and what it isn't – and then it has to be practised, one of the disciplines of life for Christians.

Unless otherwise stated, Bible quotations are taken from the NRSV.

1 Peace and presence

John 14:15–31

A child wakes during the night and calls out. The parent comes and bad dreams are dispelled with soothing words and a reassuring touch. In a crisis we call 999 and ask for the emergency services and long for the moment they arrive. Fear can come in many guises, but the inbreaking of peace most often begins with presence.

And there's the rub! The disciples are aware, vaguely, that Jesus is leaving them and already they can sense things are changing. He has said he'll ask his heavenly Father to send another, the Spirit of truth (vv. 16–17), but they don't want 'another'. He seeks to reassure them, saying of this Spirit, 'You know him, because he abides with you, and he will be in you' (v. 17). The meanings of these words are complex. Scholars aren't sure whether the words suggest the Spirit was *in* them or *beside* them, whether the Spirit's presence was present reality or future promise, relating to the Pentecost to come. But the promise was firm: 'The Father will send [him] in my name' (v. 26). And the outcome is unmistakeable: 'Peace I leave with you; my peace I give to you. I do not give to you as the world gives. Do not let your hearts be troubled, and do not let them be afraid' (v. 27).

For all the debate about these verses, what we can be sure of is how they apply to *us*, in our post-Pentecost experience. At our moment of new-birth awakening, the Holy Spirit of God is not just with us, but *within* us (v. 17), and 'on that day you will know that I am in my Father, and you in me, and I in you' (v. 20). Like a Russian doll, the Spirit is within you, you are in Christ and Christ is in the Father (see also Colossians 3:3).

We cannot help but be struck by Jesus' self-identification with the Holy Spirit, whom, he says, is in us (v. 17) – but then Jesus also says, 'I [am] in you' (v. 20). Here, then, is a mystery of great importance, laid bare before our eyes. Today it matters not how you feel or what you may be experiencing – the first thing is to understand that Jesus is with us, by his Spirit. We do not face life's anxieties alone. This is so reassuring, but we can't stop here – for God's peace is not just for you and me, but for all of creation.

2 The peace of God and the redemption of creation

Leviticus 26

The book of Leviticus sometimes gets a bad press, with various verses ripped out of context with the supposed aim of proving some point or other. But within it are gems of scripture, not least the promises of peace enshrined in today's verses. God's call to loyalty from his people – to worship him alone (v. 1), to live according to the pattern he has established (v. 2) and to follow his decrees and commands (v. 3) – sets the benchmark against which sometimes, when we depart from these things, life gets out of kilter. And I don't just mean our personal lives, but the whole of life for the whole of creation.

Interestingly, here, a vision of God's peace is not expressed in terms of good feelings but in terms of good provision. The promise of rain to yield crops and fruit (v. 4) and year-round harvests (v. 10) implies the absence of food insecurity, which still impacts billions around the world today as well as those for whom food banks have become their lifeline. The promises to 'live securely in your land' (v. 5), that 'no one shall make you afraid' and that 'no sword shall go through your land' (v. 6) speak volumes to communities in war zones today, as well as those who live in our cities where they fear for their children's safety because of knife violence, gangs or drugs. There is the gift of generation succeeding to generation in this way, each blessed by God (v. 9), and at the heart of the community will be the recognised presence of God; indeed, their very identity will be that of God's people (vv. 11–12). Yes, there are implications if they choose not to live this way (vv. 14–39), but even then, the offer of forgiveness and restoration is never withdrawn. There is always a way back (vv. 40–46).

As we begin to understand that God offers all of humankind his peace, we also see that he longs for all things to experience this shalom. In recent years, it has rightly been emphasised that just as Genesis 1 begins with the creation of all things, so Revelation 21—22 ends with the restoration of all things. Yes, peace is available to me, but its scope embraces my neighbour, my enemy and the stranger. It encompasses the sea and sky free from pollutants, the soils and rivers able to generate and regenerate, and verdant forests breathing like the lungs of the world: the whole of creation in harmony, at peace. So is there no limit to God's peace? This is where we turn to next.

3 The cross for 'all things'

Colossians 1:1–20

Today's passage offers rich food for hungry souls. After the opening sections, where Paul makes clear his affection for the Colossian Christians, he sweeps majestically through descriptions of Christ as completely embodying God (vv. 15, 19), as creator of *all things* (v. 16) and as one who existed before *all things* and who holds *all things* together (v. 17). He is the head of the church, the first fruits of the resurrection to come (v. 18), the pre-eminent one sat at God's right hand and the healer and reconciler of *all things* that are at enmity with God (v. 20). This stress on 'all things' persuades some to see this passage as offering a universalist hope, yearning for a simple symmetry between the 'all things' God has created in and through Jesus and the 'all things' reconciled by making peace through the cross. The same Greek words used for 'all things' in verse 16 (*ta panta* created) are used in verse 20 (*ta panta* reconciled to himself), and the same root is again used twice in verse 17.

All of us will know people who live without the outward evidence of a relationship with God, and our hearts cradle the hope that God will still include them. They can be friends and family, or they can be the billions who follow other faiths or no faith or who have never heard the gospel in a meaningful way. The hope that God's love is more inclusive than we can imagine is one I treasure and in which I have absolute confidence. Conversely, I recoil from the cold efficiency with which some Christians seem able to decree who will and won't be saved. To anyone who asks, I tell them with confidence the way to the Father. Anything else is God's business.

But if I was to say I am a universalist, I could only do so in the sense that Christ's reconciling death on the cross makes it *possible* for all things to be reconciled to himself. All of humanity, all of creation, all in the visible and invisible world – whether angels, principalities or powers – nothing is incapable of being reconciled. But some may not. Indeed, Jesus spoke of some who will 'go away into eternal punishment' (Matthew 25:46). Peace is offered, but peace may not ultimately be chosen.

What is certain is that the cross changed everything. Thereafter peace with God and peace in our lived experience became possible, and the first fruits of this came just three days later, this time focused on an empty tomb.

4 The first fruit of God's peace

At times we may allow our identity to be subsumed by another so that what they achieve enables us to enjoy the same outcome. For example, novice skydivers will strap themselves to a trained parachutist, a blind athlete will tie their wrist to a sighted runner and, in some artistic fields, an apprentice works under the name of their tutor.

The cross was a solitary event, never to be repeated (v. 10). What was to be done was accomplished by Jesus alone, and the declaration that 'it is finished' (John 19:30) was unequivocal. The resurrection is different; Jesus was the first to rise to new life, but others will follow. Christ endured the cross so that we *don't* have to do the same, but he rose to new life precisely in order that we *can* do the same. This is why a full-immersion baptism, when someone goes down into the water, is a poignant moment of identification. We are 'buried with him by baptism into death' and 'just as Christ was raised from the dead… we too might walk in newness of life' (v. 4).

The cross is where the peace of God was won. It demands our allegiance through an act of faith (Romans 5:1) but also through a life that is resistant to the ongoing tyranny of sin (vv. 12–14). Resurrection therefore is the first expression of a new creation characterised by God's restoration of shalom. While the finished work of Christ on the cross slams the door on all that destroyed God's plans for his creation, resurrection throws open the door to a renewed life that stretches before us, a life that will one day make manifest all that God wants us to enjoy.

The challenge for us is that we do not yet live at the point in history when the fullness of Christ's victory is realised. So our task in these in-between years, between Christ on earth and Christ's return, is to first enjoy, then proclaim and demonstrate, the fact that the cross and resurrection have changed everything, that God's peace is available now, that shalom can find expression wherever the rule of Christ finds expression. We can do this, not in and of ourselves, but because our identity is now wedded to that of Christ. Verse 11 calls us to identify fully with Christ in being dead to the sin he destroyed but alive to God in Christ, as a new creation.

5 Peace and contentment

Over the past 20 years, I have bought and sold, saved for and splashed out on various cameras and lenses, sometimes with the illusion that the photographers' Shangri-La – the perfect kit – is just one purchase away. It isn't; it's a mirage. I need to be content, for contentment is one element of peace.

Matthew 6 is, in many ways, a manifesto for personal peace. Do good but not for show (v. 1). Give generously but do it discreetly (vv. 2–4). Pray constantly but do it privately (vv. 5–7). Fast also, but don't draw attention to it (vv. 16–18). These pearls of wisdom have one thing in common – we're not to place ourselves at the centre, as if the unquenchable thirst for praise and attention from others will bring us contentment. Rather, Jesus tells us to turn away from these things and live as if God is our sole audience. That way, we won't be craving more, addicted to the applause of others, investing our lives in the mirage that one day we will have enough.

Jesus turns the table and says instead that we should store up treasures in heaven. Forget what's illusory and temporary (v. 19) and instead attend to what's real and permanent (v. 20). Why? Because our ability to choose aright dictates where our heart will lead us (v. 21). And here, it's our eyes that matter most – for with them we see and choose to give attention to either the healthy or the unhealthy (vv. 22–23). To see is one thing, but to be held captive by what we see is another. There is a choice to be made, and it isn't just one lens or one 'whatever' over against another. At its root, it's a choice of God or wealth (*mammon* in Greek) – either way, it's a word for choosing an idol (v. 24).

This is not to say that material things are of no importance. They provide life's essentials and sometimes life's luxuries. But there is no end to 'things', so we have to decide when enough is enough. Truth be told, if you are poor you are more likely to be striving for necessities. But if you are wealthy, the greater challenge is to accept that you have enough and determine to give away generously. 'But what about the need to retain wealth for an uncertain future?' I hear some say, and that's a good and reasonable question. But before you answer it in too convenient a way, take a moment to read verses 25–34 also. You may find help there.

6 Living in the experience of peace

In my 2018 book, *The Prince of Peace in a World of Wars*, I looked at instances of how biblical characters found a measure of peace even in trying circumstances. Hannah desperate for a child or Peter having his world turned upside down were two examples. I wanted to avoid giving the impression that 'real' saints are never troubled. In my experience, peace coexists with turmoil – and the turmoil is real, but God's peace is stronger and will sustain us.

In today's passage, the psalm is structured as a troubled conversation between David (vv. 1, 3, 6–8) and God (vv. 2, 4–5). The setting is evening, often the time we brood over matters that disturb or anger us. David begins in verse 1 by affirming God's past faithfulness: 'You gave me room [i.e. you heard me] when I was in distress.' Note, then, that he has been distressed before and openly acknowledges it. This is pastorally important, for as Christians we are not impervious to life's struggles. God's presence in our life is not a vaccine against problems, but it is the resource that enables us to prevent them stealing our equilibrium. As David calls, 'O God of my right' (v. 1), he affirms his trust in God as the upholder of justice.

In verse 2, David gives voice to God's response, and we detect a faint tone of censure or a sadness at David's inability to trust God in all circumstances. David affirms God's loyalty to his people (v. 3), and God tells him that in his disturbance ('anger' is better here), do not sin (v. 4) – perhaps distant echoes from elsewhere of, among other things, the call to love our enemy (Matthew 5:44) or put away the sword (John 18:11). Above all – trust God (v. 5)!

In verse 6, David speaks on behalf of those who demand that God should 'show up' in times of struggle: an understandable sentiment, but verse 7 captures perfectly the inward peace that David concedes he has come to know (v. 7a) compared to the outward and fleeting sense of well-being that comes from things like food and wine (v. 7b). As a result, he will 'lie down and sleep in peace'. The final word in verse 8 translated 'in safety' is better rendered 'unafraid'. Perhaps this, above all, is the peace we need in today's world: the absence of fear as we confront concerns about our troublesome world, our health and our families, and maybe concerns too that those we love do not know this prince of peace for themselves.

Guidelines

- A lot that I've written about peace is grounded in this notion of the presence of God with us, Christ by his Spirit in us. This is beyond our full understanding, so take a minute or two to meditate on this. Open your heart and mind to God and 'bathe in mystery'. God is with you right now.

- If a friend asked you how your faith helps you in times of trouble, how would you respond? To what degree would your replay be subjective, based on your feelings, or objective, based on what God has done? Both are valid. Both are needed.

- Can you recall times when your faith has really helped you through difficulties? Are you aware of people who might need such help now?

- How content are you? There may be valid reasons for discontent, such as poor health or concerns about loved ones. But is there a discontent that you need to lose? What underlies it?

- How easy or hard do you find it to be financially generous? What lies behind your answer?

- Take a moment to pray about any areas in which you want to see change.

1 Peace and the mission of God

Luke 1:57–80

This week we turn from an understanding of peace to its application. What place does peace play in the mission of God and, by inference, what role should it play in the mission of the church?

The birth of John the Baptist was seen by 'neighbours and relatives' (v. 58) as a sign of God's mercy (v. 58), but little did they grasp the scale of this blessing, though some perhaps sensed that this child was different (v. 66). Zechariah's prophecy was spoken over his newborn son, maybe even as he held him in his arms, the most intimate of moments. His spiritual insight is striking as he confidently connects God's faithfulness, the birth of his child, the coming Christ and God's salvation plan.

He begins by recognising that God has been gracious, has redeemed his people, just as he promised of old (vv. 68–71). The foundational covenant given to Abraham has been fulfilled (vv. 72–75). Only then does he turn his attention to his son and affirms him as a prophet called of God, one who will go before the Lord (v. 76) and baptise others for the forgiveness of their sins (v. 77). And then the finale. Already mention has been made of the birth of a Saviour (v. 69). Now we are told where all this will lead us – the sun will rise, darkness will be dispelled and this new day will 'guide our feet into the way of peace' (vv. 78–79).

We can extrapolate this account of the mission of God to help us envisage the mission of the servant church. The same confidence that God has acted decisively is required of us, a confidence in the story that also began for us with Abraham, for we too are people of the book. At the heart of our faith is the birth of a child, the prince of peace and Saviour. Now we, as his prophets, his witnesses, his ambassador, both proclaim and work for God's peace, for the shalom of God restores all that was lost when sin destroyed the peace of paradise.

Zechariah did not proclaim John to be a saviour, but a prophet, a preparer of the way, a proclaimer of knowledge and understanding (vv. 76–77). Likewise, we have no power to save, but we will declare the name of the one who does. And we will enable people to experience a greater measure of life in all its fullness, that shalom which entails food and shelter, security and a life of dignity that we saw in Leviticus earlier.

2 Peace and our deepest convictions

In my own Baptist tradition, we sometimes speak of the church as 'communities of conviction'. The description captures something of our early history and the costliness of standing firm for those things believed among us and of trusting in God even in the face of persecution. Sometimes our inability to live fully in peace, within God's purposes, is because we are not able to trust him as we should. Persecution is the experience of millions of Christians today, people of deep conviction, needing us to pray for them and support them.

Today's extract from Paul's prison letter to Timothy is deeply emotional. Paul is in prison (v. 8), in Rome (v. 17), and he writes to someone he dearly loves (v. 2; see also vv. 3–5). But the purpose of his letter is primarily focused on the gospel he entrusts again to Timothy, encouraging him to fan into flames that which was given to him (v. 6). He reminds him of the power, love and self-discipline that are gifts from God (v. 7) and the need to safeguard the teaching entrusted to him (vv. 13–14).

Notwithstanding his confinement, he talks of these things as if oblivious to his circumstances. Is he in a state of denial? Certainly not! He writes, we imagine, from a dark, damp dungeon with little fresh air, the poorest of food and all too aware by now that his life is soon to end. It is surely not a flight of fancy to see him dirty, unkempt, his hair long and straggly. Indeed, he praises Onesiphorus precisely because he wasn't ashamed of Paul when he found him in chains (v. 16).

But from such squalor and this place of apparent defeat, Paul declares his deepest conviction. 'I am not ashamed,' he says, 'for I know the one in whom I have put my trust, and I am sure that he is able to guard until that day what I have entrusted to him' (v. 12). Here, then, is Paul's anchor point, driven deep into the rock of his security – here is what holds me, here is my protection against the storm, here is my unshakeable hope in the face of death: 'because I know whom I have believed, and am convinced…' (v. 12, NIV). This is why, also from a prison cell, Paul can write to the Philippians of the peace 'which surpasses all understanding' (Philippians 4:7). Pray today for Christians who face persecution, yet long for the peace of Christ to be made real.

3 Promoting the peace of Christ

Ephesians 2

Peace is available to us, but we are also called to be peacemakers (Matthew 5:9), to declare God's peace to a troubled world and to give expression to it in practical ways. For activists like me, this is a call to arms, and my inclination can be to rush off and do something. But today's text reveals something foundational that we do well to reflect on first. Paul is writing to Ephesian Christians who are Gentiles. As such, they had often been viewed as enemies of God. To Jews like Paul, who saw themselves as God's people (see Genesis 17:7–8; Exodus 19:5; Deuteronomy 14:2; Psalm 135:4), Gentiles were historically 'not... God's people' (1 Peter 2:10).

But in and through Christ that all changed, and the basis of the change was not a redrawing of national boundaries but the inbreaking of God's grace (v. 8). They were once 'without Christ... strangers to the covenants of promise, having no hope and without God' (v. 12). Now 'in Christ Jesus' those who were 'far off have been brought near' (v. 13), for 'he is our peace' (v. 14), bringing Jews and Gentiles together and thereby 'making peace' (v. 15).

I stress this because our desire to share the peace of Christ cannot be realised without bringing the person of Christ into the equation. Without Christ, we can bring sanctified common sense, human energy and professional skills to marriage difficulties, business disputes or war zones, but we will not be able to offer the peace of Christ. Counsellors, arbitrators and those trained in conflict resolution have a hugely valuable role to play, but the prince of peace adds immeasurably more to situations we may be involved with.

Bringing Christ into the equation does not mean that everyone we speak to will become a Christian, but it's important that we are open about the inspiration and model that drives us. Our belief is in one humanity, the affirmation of each other as brothers and sisters with one heavenly Father. We recognise that their plight is also my plight, and maybe their plight is in part my fault. Just as Christ 'proclaimed peace to you who were far off and... to those who were near' (v. 17), our witness will do likewise. Our goal is to see the other as 'no longer strangers and aliens' but 'members of the household of God' (v. 19). This will take practice, patience and understanding. Above all else, it will take grace.

4 Peace and righteous anger

People tend to think of peace most naturally as a feeling, but it's also an objective reality. It either exists, even in part, or it doesn't. That's true in our own lives (see Romans 5:1) and also in the lives of others, and its absence sometimes cries out for an angry response. Peace and justice always go together, as in Isaiah 9:6–7, where we're told the prince of peace will rule with justice. So a corrupt government should cause people to rise up and demand change.

The all-too-frequent death of mothers in childbirth in developing countries demands the provision of healthcare. The presence of injustice, which is the absence of peace, demands righteous anger.

'Gentle Jesus, meek and mild' was not the Jesus who went up to Jerusalem in our reading. What he saw deeply angered him. It happened to be people selling animals for sacrifice, but there's likely evident corruption going on too. Commentators suggest that the animals people brought were routinely rejected so they had to buy others from sanctioned traders, no doubt at inflated cost. Moneychangers traded foreign currency for distant travellers so that offerings could be made in shekels, an easy opportunity for exchange rates to deprive the already poor. Each instance represented an unjust barrier to the temple achieving its primary purpose, to be a place of encounter with God, and Jesus was – and is – in the barrier-dismantling business. The outcome was a roughly fashioned whip, an overturning of tables and the driving out of those who had desecrated a holy place (vv. 15–16).

Now, I'm not making a plea for faux anger. Sometimes our response to injustice will be to grieve or pray or repent of our own complicity. The only inappropriate response to injustice is apathy, for to walk away is not a gospel option (Luke 10:31–32). But what to do in the face of major problems? We feel so inadequate.

A Sri Lankan friend of mine once lamented that millions of people live under tyrannical dictators and long for the freedoms we have. So why, he asked, do people in the west not exercise their freedom and protest to their governments? 'You're free to do so, but you take it for granted,' he said. The lesson surely is that we do something with our anger. We can act, write, pray, protest, petition, give or go and get involved. But we must not turn away. That is to acquiesce to the injustice around us.

5 Peace and personal responsibility

'If it is possible, so far as it depends on you, live peaceably with all' (v. 18). I love the realism of this text, recognising that sometimes there is only so much we can do. But before we think this lets us off the hook, for it's easy to say we've done all we could, note all what precedes this verse.

Romans 12 is addressed primarily to Christians in the local church about their interrelationships, but if we want to live consistently, it can rightly be applied beyond the church also. 'Present your bodies as a living sacrifice' (v. 1) deliberately parallels the animal sacrifices of old. In other words, how we live is our offering to God. We are told not to conform to contemporary norms (v. 2), a reminder that how we respond to situations should be countercultural. Start by being humble (vv. 3, 16), recognising that people are all different, but all necessary and all of value (vv. 4–8).

Verse 9 tells us to not just speak of love but to practise it, and verses 10–13 give us real-life examples of how we might do that. But being countercultural demands more than the evident goodness of supporting the poor and welcoming strangers (v. 13). We are actually to bless those who hurt us; this is said multiple times so we don't misunderstand it (vv. 14, 20–21). Show empathy towards others (v. 15) and even turn the other cheek (v. 17), just as Jesus said we are to do (Matthew 5:39, 43–44). Only then, only when we have examined ourselves in the light of these injunctions, might we be able to say that as far as possible we have tried everything to live peaceably with all.

Today, reading these *Guidelines*, you may be aware of those with whom you are not living peaceably. If so, have you done all you can to build the peace? If you have, keep trying but leave the rest to God (v. 19), even though strained relationships can bring untold stress and strain and a deep sadness. Even if you are in the right (with the assumption that others are wrong), how can verses 14 and 20 help you? Oh, and don't focus on the heaping of burning coals upon their heads, however tempting that may be, but on how you can bless them!

And if by God's good grace you are not experiencing struggles like this, pause and be thankful. But save this scriptural wisdom in the storehouse of life, for one day it may help you, or help you to help someone else.

6 Peace now, peace yet to come

The plaintive cry from the back seat of the car, 'Are we there yet?', will be familiar to all who have transported children. When it comes to our desire to live in the peace of God, and further, to see God's peace transforming our broken world, that cry is ours too. One thing is for sure – we *aren't* there yet, and here's the brutal truth: we never will be until Christ returns. That is a heavy burden to carry, and emotive texts like today's psalm capture our anguish as we long for change.

David has kept his mouth shut until now (v. 1), but his distress has increased until his heart burns within him (vv. 2–3). So he finally speaks, or shouts, at God. 'Tell me when I die' captures his longing to escape this life (vv. 4–6). Today, your life may or may not be in tumult, but the world certainly is, so this is surely a cry for a world that never seems to find rest. But David realises that he still has a choice: he can succumb to his despair, or he can turn again to God in whom he hopes (v. 7). His immediate concern is against those he calls 'the fool' (v. 8), and he attributes their injustices towards him to be the direct result of God allowing it to happen (vv. 9–10), maybe as a punishment for sin, perhaps even David's own sin (v. 11).

The last two verses bring David back again to that familiar place – he has nowhere else to run, no one else to trust. Even in despair, it's God alone who offers hope. David's longing is for peace, but he concedes that he is like the sojourner within Israel's borders, with no entitlement to land, dependent on the kindness of others. He too is just a 'passing guest', entirely at the mercy of God (v. 12). We glimpse the heartbreaking tension between the hopeful refrain, 'Hear my prayer, O Lord' (v. 12), and the hopeless 'turn your gaze away from me' (v. 13), akin to Peter's 'Go away from me, Lord, for I am a sinful man!' (Luke 5:8).

Peace *has* been won through Christ's death and resurrection, and every step we take to share the peace of God in today's world declares that truth. But we also live in this place of tension between what is and what is yet to be. In that place, on this day, don't despair. Turn to God and speak with the searing honesty that David demonstrates here. God can take it!

Guidelines

- Do you consider yourself to be a person of conviction? The answer will surely be yes, but how would you describe those convictions to an enquiring friend? Without using religious language, what is the heart of your faith?

- I fully expect that readers of *Guidelines* will be as active as they can be in their church. But can you think of activities undertaken by your church where the beneficiaries would rarely hear of Christ? Why might that be? Are there circumstances when that is appropriate?

- From childhood, we are told that anger is a negative emotion, and of course it can be. What distinguishes destructive anger and righteous anger? Are there things that make you angry? How does that show? How can you channel that anger for good?

- This tension between 'now' and 'not yet' – does it help or hinder your faith? Can you say why? Can you describe real-life examples?

FURTHER READING

David Kerrigan, *The Prince of Peace in a World of Wars: Applying the message of God's love to a needy world* (BRF, 2018).

Ian M. Randall, *Communities of Conviction: Baptist beginnings in Europe* (Neufeld Verlag, 2009).

Ian Stackhouse, *Praying Psalms: A personal journey through the psalter* (Cascade Books, 2018).

Old Testament texts for Christmas

David Spriggs

The annual service of Nine Lessons and Carols from King's College Cambridge has become a national institution; indeed, it celebrated its centenary in 2018. Many other churches up and down the land have emulated this prestigious service – often with candlelit services. While the quality of singing in these services may not quite reach the heights of the choristers at King's, the scripture readings are frequently very similar.

It is fascinating to note that while the music and carols in the King's College service vary year by year, the biblical passages remain the same. The Old Testament ones are Genesis 3 and 22 and Isaiah 9 and 11. The New Testament ones also allude to other passages, such as Isaiah 7 and Micah 5.

In these notes, we will explore some of these Old Testament passages, consider their significance in the places in the New Testament where they are quoted or alluded to, and reflect on their significance for deepening our understanding of the Christmas events today.

The intention of these notes is to deepen our appreciation of these passages in their biblical contexts and so extend and enrich our awareness of the biblical voices in this traditional service. Often, the various carols and songs we sing, as well as the prayers and reflections offered, add interpretations and insights to our total experience.

We can perhaps approach this richly textured experience along the lines of a musical composition. The New Testament story provides the melody, the carols and reflections the harmony and the Old Testament the descant.

Unless otherwise stated, Bible quotations are taken from the NRSV.

1 The problem and the promise

Genesis 3:8–19

There are several points we can make to commend this as the first of the readings in Nine Lessons and Carols. Fundamentally it puts the story, which will focus on one baby born in a remote part of the Roman empire, in a universal context. Its backdrop is, of course, the creation of the universe and the creation of man and woman in God's image and likeness. This is followed by the disobedience of Eve and Adam, initiated by the serpent's insinuating conversation with Eve. To summarise, then, God's beautiful creation and his special representatives to take care of it are now all corrupted. Animals are alienated from humans, man and woman are alienated from each other and all are alienated from God, the source of their life. 'Cursed are you among all animals… Cursed is the ground because of you' (vv. 14, 17).

Childbearing, for the woman, and the care for creation, for the man, have now become hard labour with frustration, instead of the proper, natural expression of our humanity with great fruitfulness.

But the problem for the biblical scholar is that the verse which seems to have messianic connotations – 'He will strike your head, and you will strike his heel' (v. 15) – is most naturally understood as describing a state of fear, animosity and intent to kill between all Eve's descendants and all snakes. Yet through much of Christian history it has been perceived as the 'first gospel proclamation', as Luther put it. This goes back at least as far as Irenaeus, Bishop of Lyon, around 180 AD. This sees in the snake the work of Satan and in the offspring Jesus.

While many biblical commentators see here only an explanation of the felt fear between humans and actual snakes, we do need to recognise the fundamental role attributed to the snake in Genesis 3, namely the arch-tempter. It is therefore understandable that people would make the link to Satan. Once this is done, the identification of Jesus to the offspring easily follows. Those ancient commentators helpfully remind us of this dimension to the story.

2 God's choice of Abraham to bless the nations

Genesis 22:15–18

This passage begins by telling us the angel of the Lord spoke 'a second time from heaven' (v. 15). The first occasion was a few verses earlier, where this angel had stopped Abraham from sacrificing his son Isaac. This context is presumably one reason why this account of God's blessing Abraham is preferred in this service to the first one in Genesis 12:1–3 which, viewed in the light of Advent, has another resonance.

In Genesis 12:1 we read, 'Go from your country and your kindred and your father's house.' We know from archaeology that Abram's birthplace of Ur was a significant centre of early civilisation. From here, with his father Terah, Abram moved to Haran. Haran also was a highly developed commercial city and was founded by the Third Dynasty of Ur. It was a centre for the worship of the moon cult of Babylon. Hence the call of God was a call to leave a prestigious centre for a very uncertain future. Abram's departure from Haran involved a significant loss of status, security and civilising comforts. This echoes one of the themes of the hymn in Philippians 2:7–8, where it says that Christ Jesus 'emptied himself... humbled himself'.

The context of Genesis 22 reminds us of the other dimension of Philippians 2:8, namely that 'he became obedient to the point of death'. Although in Genesis 22 it is 'to the point of' Isaac's death, within the context of the Abraham stories this also implied a kind of death for Abraham, for it was through Abraham's son Isaac that God's promise of multiple blessings was to be fulfilled. It must have seemed to Abraham that he no longer had the future promised by God.

It is the promised blessings which may be seen to justify the inclusion of this passage in the service. Why is that? Verse 18 provides the major clue: 'By your offspring shall all the nations of the earth gain blessing for themselves.' Although in context 'offspring' is likely to be read as plural ('as numerous as... the sand that is on the seashore', v. 17), it can also be understood, in the context of Christ's coming, as referring to Jesus, the one through whom all nations will find their ultimate blessing. Simeon was to express it like this, 'For my eyes have seen your salvation, which you have prepared in the presence of all peoples, a light for revelation to the Gentiles' (Luke 2:30–32).

3 Light in darkness

Isaiah 9:1-7

Although in Luke 2:30-32 Simeon does not quote Isaiah 9:2, he certainly echoes it. In Isaiah, the people who sit in darkness live in 'Galilee of the nations' (v. 1) and 'on them light has shined' (v. 2). Matthew is much more direct in quoting this passage, but he refers it not to Christ's birth but to the start of his ministry in Galilee (Matthew 4:15-16). These two New Testament references show us that the Isaiah passage was connected to the gospel story in the minds of the early Christian communities.

In its historical context, these verses may have related to either the birth (as with Isaiah 7:10-17) or the accession to the throne (see Psalm 2) of Hezekiah or Josiah (see for example Clements, *Isaiah 1—39*, pp. 103-109). What is more significant for us is that this passage seems to reflect the more general language that would be used on such occasions. To try to find one specific historical event may well miss the point the New Testament writers are making. These verses, and similar songs relating to the king, had what we can describe as an ambitious or even extravagant nature (see Psalm 72). Some have described this 'extra' as idealism. We can consider that they had an anticipatory component which originally expressed Israel's hopes for their new king, but which carried with them elements that fuelled messianic hopes too.

The resonance for our Advent is not restricted to these elements, however. Far more prominent are the words 'For a child has been born for us' (v. 6) and the titles/descriptions which follow: 'Wonderful Counsellor, Mighty God, Everlasting Father, Prince of Peace.' This 'child' is the fulfilment of the hopes piled on to David and his successors. These hopes in a multitude of ways were attached to Jesus – not only his lineage and birth (e.g. Matthew 1:1-17; 2:5-6) but also his ministry.

Of equal significance, but not as much noted, is the claim in Isaiah that 'the zeal of the Lord of hosts will do this' (v. 7). Here is the prophetic assurance that, contrary to contemporary events and future circumstances, these promises will be fulfilled, because they depend not on human initiative or even on obedience, but on God's nature.

4 A new David?

This is the third potential reference to a coming 'new-style king' in Isaiah in a few chapters. Each contributes something distinctive to the hope expressed in this book.

The context within the Isaianic material is that of Isaiah 10:24–27. Here, God promises an end to his judgement on Israel and Judah carried out by the Assyrians – 'his burden will be removed from your shoulder' (10:27).

A key distinctive of Isaiah 11 is that it refers not to a son of David, that is, a descendant from the Davidic kingship line, but to 'a shoot… from the stock of Jesse' (v. 1), implying that God is going to make a new beginning, going behind David's only family to start again. While the reference to 'the stock of Jesse' might imply a rejection of the Davidic kings, it may also be a way of God saying, 'I can and will act to raise up another one like David himself.' It certainly indicates that God is capable of providing his people with a new leader, while recognising the links to the promises of an unending covenant, made to David and his family.

This leader will be endowed with God's Spirit, enabling him to negotiate effectively and distribute justice discerningly. His capabilities arise out of his relationship with God ('the fear of the Lord', v. 3). He will have a special concern for the poor and meek. His weapons may well not be militaristic but those of effective decision-making ('the rod of *his mouth*', v. 4). His word of appropriate justice will be implemented as though it were God's own. His reign will be marked by deep-level peace and security between those who are normally threatening one another and fearful of one another – even within the animal world. It is as though the anxieties which lead to conflict and danger have been drained out of the system by the exercise of wise leadership.

The reference to a little child leading them appears to be incidental rather than fundamental, as it is there not because a special child is in mind, but to show the extent of the harmony. However, it echoes in our Christian minds with Isaiah 7:14 and the birth of Jesus.

This passage concludes with the promises that the whole earth (world) will overflow with 'the knowledge of the Lord' (v. 9). This can be taken not only as knowledge of what God wants, including his commandments, but as knowing God himself – a restored relationship with him.

5 An origin from of old

Micah 5:2, with its reference to Bethlehem, is perhaps the second most prominent prophecy associated with the Christmas stories. It is prominent in Matthew's gospel, and the story of the Magi and the flight into Egypt revolve around it. It is prominent in many carols, and it is hard to imagine a traditional nativity play without the core element of the birth of Jesus in Bethlehem.

We do well to remember, however, that this verse is part of a bigger context. Micah 4:11–13 describes a situation where Jerusalem is being attacked or besieged, and the enemy is confident of victory. In words reminiscent of Isaiah 40—55, the prophet explains that the enemy does not understand the plans of God, which are to do good to Israel and destroy those who attack her.

In contrast to a besieged Jerusalem, the verse from Micah quoted by Matthew speaks of a new ruler coming from Bethlehem, as King David did, but it also indicates some tension with the normal Davidic kingship motifs. It suggests that this new ruler will go back behind the direct Davidic line when it states, 'whose origins are from of old' (5:2). In this way, this prophecy concurs with Isaiah 11:1. As there, so here: we are next provided with an aspirational description of the ruler's role as shepherd of his people, who provides security for them. This ruler will gain extensive recognition and be the source of Israel's peace. But he does this not in his own strength, wisdom or wealth, but by God's empowerment.

As we recall the Old Testament context for the well-known New Testament passage, several things resonate with Jesus, in addition to his place of birth. There is his connection to but also priority over David himself. There is his role as shepherd of Israel, which was normally attributed to God himself (e.g. Psalm 95:6–7) but which Jesus drew to himself (see John 10:11–18 and compare Matthew 9:35–36; Hebrews 13:20; 1 Peter 2:25). Finally, we may highlight that he is the source of peace and that his reign is not marked by military victories.

6 Emmanuel

Matthew 1:18–25; Isaiah 7:10–17

This prophecy that 'the virgin shall conceive and bear a son' who will be called Emmanuel (Matthew 1:23; compare Isaiah 7:14) is probably at the same time the best-known and the most contentious of Old Testament prophecies related to the birth of Jesus. Often this is seen as one of the most convincing evidences of the reality of Old Testament prophecy. Such an amazing prediction 700 years before it happened is seen to underline the Christian doctrine of the virgin birth of Jesus. There are, however, a number of issues we need to note if we are to do justice to both the New Testament use of this passage and the Old Testament passage itself.

We begin with Matthew's reference to Emmanuel. From this, we can note that Matthew shows us that he is not bound to a very literal understanding of the Old Testament quotation. That passage unequivocally states that this son will be named Emmanuel. Matthew explains this Hebrew word for his Greek readers – it means 'God is with us' (1:23). More significantly, he has already told us that in fact this new baby will not be called Emmanuel but 'Jesus, for he will save his people from their sins' (1:21), and this is underlined by the claim that Joseph named him Jesus (1:25). The Old Testament passage and the surrounding context make it clear that the actual name the child was given (not simply its meaning or implication) was important. Yet for Matthew this was not the case. The significance triumphed over literalism.

So what of Isaiah's 'virgin birth'? We have already noted that Matthew thoughtfully translates his Hebrew quotations (including this one) into Greek. As is often the case, the Hebrew and the Greek translations are not exact equivalents. The English 'virgin' is an appropriate translation of the Greek *parthenos*. However, in Genesis 34:3–4, *parthenos* is used when it is clear the female concerned is not a virgin – she has been raped. The semantic emphasis for the equivalent word in the Hebrew is on her being female and youthful. So she may or may not be a virgin (obviously she could well be, because she is young).

While in the Isaiah passage the emphasis is on the name (Emmanuel) not the virginal birth, it is clear that for Matthew (and Luke) this was an important reality, which Matthew sees prefigured in the Old Testament.

Guidelines

- How does reading the Old Testament passages which are referred to in the New Testament affect your understanding? Consider where it has enriched your rereading of the Advent and Christmas stories? Where has it served as a distraction?

- How might you share some of the Old Testament understanding presented here with the congregation attending a traditional Nine Lessons and Carols service?

- Reflect on some traditional carols which echo these Old Testament passages. Do you think they communicate either the Old Testament or New Testament meanings, or do they reflect more the cultural contexts in which they were written?

FURTHER READING

R.E. Clements, *Isaiah 1—39 (NCBC)* (Marshall, Morgan & Scott, 1980).
John Goldingay, *Genesis for Everyone (Part 1)* (SPCK, 2010).
I. Howard Marshall, *The Gospel of Luke* (Paternoster, 1979).
Leon Morris, *The Gospel according to Matthew* (IVP, 1992).

The Bible 20:20

Paul Williams

We live in a time when ignorance of the Bible is on the rise. Bible Society research suggests that increasing numbers of children no longer hear or read Bible stories and that a startling 25% of adults believe Superman is in the Bible. Ignorance is a breeding ground for fear, prejudice and contempt. Hostile attitudes towards the Bible are frequently voiced, and those who adhere to or speak from the Bible are increasingly mocked or shamed as bigots.

It is easy for Christians to become judgemental or reactive in response to this. But we would do well first to remove the log from our own eyes before pointing out the speck in others'. Sadly, the evidence shows that Bible ignorance and distrust is rife *within* the church, not just outside of it. Sixty per cent of millennial Christians find the Bible hard to relate to, and a third of all churchgoers report losing trust in it. This state of affairs is particularly damning for Protestant Christians: we have fought over the Bible and then forgotten it.

In scripture, failing to ask God for guidance is a definition of stupidity (Jeremiah 10:21). It was during the time of the Judges, when 'everyone did what was right in his own eyes' (Judges 17:6), when the priests did not know God and treated him with contempt (1 Samuel 2:12–17), that 'the word of the Lord was rare' (1 Samuel 3:1) and finally the 'glory [of God] departed from Israel' (1 Samuel 4:21–22).

This combination of spiritual pride and God's absence can take a legalistic as well as a lawless form. Out of the long intertestamental period of longing and hoping for the messiah, one group to emerge was the Pharisees, convinced that detailed obedience to the law would bring God back. Yet Jesus saw this too as a kind of ignorance. The Pharisees were 'blind guides' (Matthew 15:14), because though they knew the detail of the law, they missed its central heart of justice, mercy, faithfulness and love (Matthew 23:23; Luke 11:42).

In this week's notes, I hope to provide some resources for considering and responding to our own cultural moment by reflecting on what the Bible says about itself and about our relationship with God's word.

Unless otherwise stated, Bible quotations are taken from the ESV.

1 'In the beginning...'

Genesis 1

In the beginning we had no scripture. Our first encounter with the word of God is in the world-creating power of God's speech. On each successive day of creation, God's words 'let there be...' command time and space; sea, land and sky; stars and planets; and animals, birds and people into being. Psalm 33:9 captures this well when it declares: 'For he spoke, and it came to be; he commanded, and it stood firm.'

A variety of Hebrew words are used to highlight not only that God's speech effects his will to bring new things into being, but also that his words name and structure reality. When God calls the light 'day', he is not simply generating luminescence but calling forth the reality of time that passes in a rhythm of day and night (vv. 3–5). In the absence of form or purpose, God's speech brings order from chaos by naming and creating a structured and purposeful design for the world. The first few verses of Psalm 19 celebrate the way that this inherent meaning in creation itself speaks back of God's glory.

My colleague Dr Craig Gay asks a delightfully intriguing question: 'What were Adam's first words?' His answer, 'I'm very well, thank you,' evokes the idea that God's speech not only creates humanity but also awakens human consciousness. Like a child learning to speak by listening to the words of a parent, God's loving speech to us establishes relationship and enables us to articulate ourselves.

As God's regents in the world, we are called to steward the earth in cooperation with God, and language is our primary tool. We are involved in naming the world, and in doing so we shape and create meaning and knowledge. Though derivative of God's power, human language has the power to build up and to tear down. We too can create realities with our words.

How will we use this power?

2 'Did God actually say?'

What is the root of all wrongdoing in the world? Genesis depicts the fall of humanity as arising not from sexual sin, not from murder and not from disbelieving in God's existence. All these sins, as bad as they may be, do not take place until after the fall has already happened. No – the root of all wrongdoing in the world arises from none of these but rather, according to scripture, from a failure to trust God's word.

These verses contain a number of archetypal elements, beginning with the serpent's question, 'Did God actually say…?' Always the evil one seeks to question and raise doubts about what God has said and about his character. The tactic to engage Eve in conversation is a deliberate false exaggeration, that God has banned eating from all trees (3:1). Eve's corrective response to the snake is accurate save in one respect: she too exaggerates by stating that God has warned them not even to *touch* the single tree in the middle of the garden (compare 3:3 with 2:17). And, imitating the snake, Eve uses only God's title as creator, not the covenant name for God found throughout the rest of this narrative (from 2:4—3:24). All this suggests that the snake is powerfully suggesting, and Eve is sympathetic to, the idea that God is rather distant and that his command is rather harsh. Forgotten in this dialogue is the lavish hospitality of God and the intimacy with him available to Adam and Eve.

Are we prone to doubt the goodness of God and wonder whether his word is not, after all, rather harsh?

Having aroused negative feelings about God and stimulated desire to disobey, the snake boldly appears to contradict what God has said. The devious nature of the snake's words become apparent when the couple heed them: they *don't* immediately die, their eyes *are* opened and God himself states that in one respect human beings have become *like* God (3:22). And yet they have nonetheless been deceived: all they see with their newly opened eyes is just how unworthy they are to be in God's presence; so, naked and ashamed, they hide from him. Physical death is now their destiny (3:19), whereas they had been offered of the fruit of the tree of life. And spiritual death occurs immediately: they are expelled from the life-giving garden sanctuary and alienated from God.

3 'If we hear the voice of the Lord our God any more, we shall die'

Deuteronomy 4:5–9, 32–35; 5:22–33

The effects of the fall – on both ruler and ruled – are powerfully symbolised for the people of Israel by their enslavement in Egypt. It is not until after God has delivered them from slavery that they are first given the words of God in writing and commanded to write them down. The writing down of 'the law' formally begins a process which eventually leads to the completion of the Hebrew Bible.

The scriptures (literally 'the writings') are certainly a gift from God to celebrate. But, before we can fully understand this gift, we need to appreciate why the written word of God is also a symbol of something terribly sad.

There is a deep tragedy in the juxtaposition of Deuteronomy 4:32–35 with the account of Adam and Eve walking and talking with God in the cool of the day. The people of Israel are literally terrified of hearing God's voice (5:25–26). They ask Moses to listen for them. Humanity's relationship with God has broken so badly that it has moved from a place of intimacy to one requiring mediation. Scripture – the written word of God – is part of God's provision of this mediation. Its purpose is to restore trust and relationship so that the effects of the fall are countered and eventually overcome. By embodying the law, Israel would become a light to the nations.

Relationship with God is restored through the written word, as it helps us trust in God, remember what he has done for us and obey his commands (see Psalm 78:1–8). Ultimately, the law was given to 'bring us unto Christ' (Galatians 3:24, KJV), the perfect mediator.

Israel's history is one of repeated cycles of disobedience, warnings and judgement followed by repentance and restoration. But disobedience is what dominates these cycles, leading ultimately to invasion, the destruction of the temple and exile. At one level, it is a thousand-year case study in how the knowledge of good and evil does not lead to life and flourishing. Despite holding the incredible gift of God's wisdom in written form, Israel seems unable to heed the warning of Deuteronomy 30:19: they cannot choose life.

4 'The Word became flesh'

The majestic opening of John's gospel takes us back to the world-creating speech of God in Genesis 1. Now, into the darkness and despair of Israel's long exile from God in their own land comes a new and better mediator between God and humanity: the Word made flesh. Jesus, by nature both divine and human, contains the very life of God. Though humanity had been expelled from the garden of Eden, and Israel had failed to live by the written word, it is as though the essence of existence in Eden and of the promised land is now present. Suddenly, human beings are face-to-face with God again. Suddenly, the tree of life is made available to us once more. Suddenly, God's presence is here, now, in the temple of the body of Jesus Christ.

When Jesus speaks, he upholds the authority of the written word, 'the Law' and 'the Prophets' that comprise the Hebrew Bible (Matthew 5:17–19), but he teaches with an authority that makes these writings about him, for him and of him (e.g. Matthew 5:21–48; Luke 24:27). He speaks with the authority of the author.

Yet, for the most part, all this is hidden from his contemporaries. The knowledge of good and evil has left even the best of them ignorant about true spiritual life (John 3:10). The teachers of the law are described by Jesus as 'blind guides' (e.g. Matthew 15:14).

There are rare moments when people suddenly have their eyes opened to Jesus' glory and divinity, and often this is associated with his words. At the transfiguration, the disciples are told by the voice from heaven, 'This is my beloved Son; listen to him!' (Mark 9:7). When the twelve disciples are asked if they too will abandon Jesus, Peter confesses Christ's divine commission and answers on behalf of them all, 'Lord, to whom shall we go? You have the words of eternal life' (John 6:68).

Peter understands that gaining or losing eternal life has something to do with words. Later in John's gospel, this concept becomes central to the powerful metaphor of the vine and the branches. Remaining in Jesus is all about his words remaining in us and we in them. The fruit of eternal life comes by trusting his words so much that they become part of us (John 15:3, 7, 10) – the exact opposite of not trusting and seeking instead to trust our own knowledge of good and evil.

5 'For the letter kills, but the Spirit gives life'

The new age of the coming kingdom commences following Jesus' crucifixion, resurrection and ascension and the outpouring of the Holy Spirit. It's a moment long anticipated by Israel's prophets. Jeremiah, Ezekiel and Isaiah all know that Israel has failed repeatedly to keep the covenant and will likely fail again. They each become messengers of God's promise of a new covenant, in which trust in God's word and obedience to the law will now be underwritten by God himself (Jeremiah 31:31–34; Ezekiel 36:25–27; Isaiah 59:21). God promises to deal with their sin, give them a new spirit and a new heart, and put his words and laws into them. All God's people will know God's ways, trust his word and be empowered to live God's way, because the same Spirit that filled Jesus will come and fill them.

The written word – the letter of the law – on its own is insufficient as a mediator between us and God. It tells us the very truth and wisdom of God, but by itself it serves only to show where we fall short. It cannot empower us to live by it. But this very characteristic can also draw us nearer to God, because it highlights our need of God – it points us to Jesus.

The language in our passage may lead some to wonder whether we need the scriptures (Hebrew or Christian) at all, now that we have the Spirit. But this would be a grave mistake. The problem is not with the scriptures but with us – it is our hardness of heart and unbelief that remains resistant to what God is saying to us. The scriptures record a series of amazing love letters between God and humanity, and our woeful misunderstanding of them, over many centuries. By the Spirit, suddenly we can see what we missed. God's wisdom and love becomes clear. Our own faithlessness and ignorance are revealed, alongside God's greater grace and mercy. Our hearts begin to 'burn within us' (Luke 24:32) as the whole Bible sharpens for us into a picture of God's glory revealed in Jesus Christ (2 Peter 1:16–21). This is why Paul can say so emphatically to Timothy, 'All Scripture is God-breathed' (2 Timothy 3:16, NIV). The written words bring us as close to God as hearing his voice whisper in our ear. The Bible is only a breath away from God: the breath of the same Spirit that comes alongside us to give life as we read.

6 'Heaven and earth will pass away, but my words will not pass away'

Revelation 21:22—22:5

When Jesus speaks of the law in Matthew 5:18, he is emphatic in saying that not even 'a dot' of its words will pass away *until* heaven and earth pass away and all things have been accomplished. Both Jeremiah 31:31–34 and Hebrews 8:8–12 make clear that the purpose of the written word is to bring us back into an intimate relationship with God, so that 'they shall all know [him]' (Hebrews 8:11). In the new creation, this mediatorial role will have been completed and fulfilled. We will no longer need to be taught to 'know the Lord', because we will all know him and see him face-to-face.

For this reason, it is no surprise that later in Matthew 24:35 we find Jesus making a more striking claim about his own words than he has made earlier about the written word of the law. Unlike the law, which will pass away eventually, Jesus' words, he says, will *not* pass away, even after the passing of the present heavens and earth. The reason is obvious – he is the resurrected living Lord, whose presence, glory and light fills the heavenly city and by whose wisdom the nations will walk. Humanity will once again have access to the tree of life, whose leaves will heal the wounds of the fall.

This biblical account of the limited purpose of the Bible only serves to heighten its importance for us today. Our eternal destiny is to live in the unmediated presence of Jesus, fully trusting his words and living by his wisdom. Whatever that new creation life is like, it involves responsibility to rule and reign and to offer the fruit of our work – our glory and honour – as worship before the throne. To live in the light of this glorious destiny now is to give ourselves, under the guidance and inspiration of the Spirit, to trusting God's written word and to building every aspect of our lives upon it. This kind of life is the best possible preparation for eternity. It requires great humility, dependence and courage. It starts when we trust the gospel invitation to repent of our sins, receive God's forgiveness in Christ and be reconciled to God. But there is no end to how deeply we can grow in our trust of Jesus, or in our knowledge of his love, or in our manifestation of his life to others.

Guidelines

This week's readings have reflected on the vital and central importance of trusting God's word for human life. Humanity needs the words of God to live in the same way that we need bread to eat. In our 'advanced', 'modern' societies (note the self-generated adjectives), we think of ourselves as wealthy, well-fed, strong and powerful. But the reality is that our rejection and neglect of scripture means that we are spiritually poor, emaciated, weak and at the mercy of hostile spiritual power. This is a description of western culture, but it is a description that in significant measure applies also to the western church. We are in a perilous state.

Josiah became king following a time of apostasy in Israel. During building works to restore the temple, the 'Book of the Law' was found and read after a time of considerable neglect. The prophetess Huldah brought God's message to Josiah that judgement for disobedience was now coming, but that his repentance and leadership would delay it (2 Kings 22).

During the Babylonian exile, even the Gentile kings recognised the need for Israel's law to be taught. There was grieving and weeping among the returned exiles when it was read aloud by Ezra the priest. But the people were told not to grieve, but to confess their sins and commit to changing their behaviour. The joy of the Lord would be their strength if they broke completely with foreign gods and all forms of syncretism (Ezra 7; Nehemiah 8—10).

During a time of persecution under Rome, Jewish Christians were tempted to compromise and turn back from Jesus to a form of faith that would attract less hostility from Roman society. But the writer of Hebrews warns them in the strongest possible terms not to turn back but to diligently apply themselves to knowing God's word and putting it into practice. Though they should be teachers, they were ignorant and immature, like infants needing milk when they should be adults eating solid food (Hebrews 5:11—6:12).

Apostasy, exile, persecution: which of these best describes our cultural moment? Would our repentance delay inevitable judgement? If we repent and stop compromising, might God rebuild and restore what has been broken down? Are we being warned not to compromise in the face of hostility, but to resolve to know and live out God's word more diligently? Either way, our next step is the same.

FURTHER READING

Craig Bartholomew and Michael Goheen, *The Drama of Scripture: Finding our place in the biblical story* (Baker Academic, 2004).

Lesslie Newbigin, *A Walk through the Bible* (SPCK, 1999).

Eugene Peterson, *Eat This Book: A conversation in the art of spiritual reading* (Eerdmans, 2006).

Guidelines forthcoming issue

HELEN PAYNTER

'Did not our heart burn within us while he talked with us on the road?' So marvelled the two disciples after that famous walk on the road to Emmaus. How often I've wished I could have eavesdropped on their conversation with Jesus! How marvellous it would be to have the whole scope of the Bible explained to us by the master; the One to whom it points.

One of the marvellous things about scripture – to me – is how endlessly contemplatable it is. Passages I know well can still leap off the page and bite me as I read. Parts that I know less well can suddenly come alive in my hands and open my eyes to new things. Scriptures join up and converse with one another, as I breathlessly look on.

In our next issue, we will be looking at scriptures that are very familiar and those that may be less so. We will contemplate again the wonders of Holy Week and Easter under the guidance of Lucy Peppiatt; we will read parts of the gospel of Mark with Steve Motyer. These are deep pools that we will never bottom out. Maybe 2 Samuel is familiar to you; I'm confident that David Firth will show you something new there.

Some parts may be less well known to you. Perhaps you aren't particularly au fait with the book of Job, or with Zechariah, or with Revelation. Alec Gilmore, Hazel Sherman and Steve Finamore will expertly guide us through some of the wonders of these books. And if you do consider yourself familiar with them – I'm pretty sure there will be new things to discover, too.

The writer to the Hebrews tells us that God's word is living and active, and so it seems indeed – a living thing that speaks back to us, that contemplates us as we contemplate it, that interrogates us. As I write, I'm finalising the edit on the January 2021 notes, and I'll be excited to put them into your hands. Maybe you'll write and tell us some of the ways that your hearts have burned within you.

Why the Bible matters to me: Rosie Button

A treasured memory: on a cool early morning in a sun-dappled clearing, with a simple oblong mud-brick church behind us and four low wooden benches drawn up in a square on the dusty dry grass, a small group of people were gathered for an hour before church to read the Bible with me. As well as wanting to practise English, they wanted to study the book of Job, because they related to it so well, and reading it with them gave me a completely different perspective. This was one of my first experiences of reading the Bible across cultures, and I relished it every week (in spite of the long walk and the unbelievably early hour!). I loved that the Bible spoke to all of us as God's people, no matter our different culture, experience or the different things we were going through. And by listening to them, I learned new things about God and his word.

I have been blessed to spend much of my working life in and around the Bible – first as an RE teacher and later teaching Old and New Testament at theological colleges in Zimbabwe and Uganda, experiencing the way the Bible applies in rural Zambia, in urban Zimbabwe, to Ugandan university students and to the technology-driven west alike. More recently I have been teaching in a missions college, thinking among other things about the biblical basis of member care, and about gender in the Bible and mission… You would think that I should know the Bible really well by now! But I still often find bits I feel like I have never read, or noticed, or understood, before. It is an exciting and living word. I am convinced we should all hear the Bible, if at all possible, through other people's voices, to learn from their perspectives and grow in our understanding.

In spite of my work being wrapped up in the Bible, it is never just an academic exercise: it is about connecting with God. Augustine of Hippo said, 'The Holy Scriptures are our letters from home,' and this resonates with me. God reaches out to communicate to us as we read his word, situated as we are in the world, not yet at home, seeking by his Spirit to understand and connect with him.

It may be a well-worn analogy, but what somebody said of John's gospel is true of the whole of scripture – it is like a great lake such that a child can play in its shallows and an elephant can swim in its depths. Sometimes I just want to paddle in the shallows and focus on a simple verse from a psalm;

other times I want to engage with a difficult passage and read commentaries and really go beneath the surface. But in either case, it is about trying to get a deeper understanding of God and connect with him.

An extract from *At Home in Advent*

Following on from the success of *At Home in Lent*, Gordon Giles takes a journey through Advent to Christmas and beyond in the company of familiar seasonal and domestic objects and experiences.

Focusing on the everyday stuff we typically associate with this time of year, including some things not so festive, he reflects on their spiritual significance, meaning and message in today's world. Beginning with chapters on journeying and travel, the book moves though major Advent themes of expectation, waiting, mortality and hope to the joy of incarnation and salvation.

The following extract is from the reflection for 20 December, entitled 'Christmas carols: missionary music'.

As God's chosen ones, holy and beloved, clothe yourselves with compassion, kindness, humility, meekness, and patience. Bear with one another and, if anyone has a complaint against another, forgive each other; just as the Lord has forgiven you, so you also must forgive. Above all, clothe yourselves with love, which binds everything together in perfect harmony. And let the peace of Christ rule in your hearts, to which indeed you were called in the one body. And be thankful. Let the word of Christ dwell in you richly; teach and admonish one another in all wisdom; and with gratitude in your hearts sing psalms, hymns, and spiritual songs to God. And whatever you do, in word or deed, do everything in the name of the Lord Jesus, giving thanks to God the Father through him.

COLOSSIANS 3:12–17 (NRSV)

At this time of year there is a very perceptible crescendo of carol singing as we approach Christmas Day. Radio stations have their sonic equivalent of the Advent calendar, increasing the Christmas flavour as the anticipation mounts, so much so that by Christmas Eve Classic FM plays little else. Strictly speaking the Christmas season begins on Christmas Eve (not 1 December), by which time many people have heard as many Christmas carols as they can bear, and by New Year's Day the Christmas music has diminished and normal service is resumed. The popular song 'The Twelve Days of Christmas' reminds us that there are twelve days after Christmas in the season, and we might remember that Christmastide evolves into Epiphanytide, which actually lasts until Candlemas on 2 February, when the church celebrates the Presentation of Christ in the Temple. The Christmas season lasts 40 days. Yet if we added that to the run-up to Christmas, we would have two months of Christmas carols!

That would be wonderful. Most Christmas carols are actually hymns of praise to God, extolling the virtues of divine love, the saving work of God and the theology of incarnation and reminding us of the biblical story. At no other time of the year do we hear so much Christian gospel in our shops, on our streets and on the airwaves. For some people, carol singing is the sound of Christmas, and even if they never darken the doors of a church, they love carols.

Many people do come to church at Christmas. Church of England statistics reveal that around 2.5 million people have attended carol services consistently over the past decade. Nine Lessons and Carols services have been held for a century now and still attract large numbers, especially if candlelit. The service provides a staple menu of Christmas hymns sung by the congregation, carols sung by a choir and readings from the Bible that tell of the 'run-up to Christmas', and it culminates with some hard-core theology, found in the final reading of John 1. Likewise the related Carols from Kings television broadcast, while not the same content as the service, attracts millions of viewers on Christmas Eve afternoon, especially for the music. These broadcasts and services in cathedrals and churches epitomise Christmas for many people.

Many Christmas carols are macaronic (sung in two languages), especially those which quote the angels' *gloria* in Latin. When church services were in Latin, the people generally did not understand much of what was said or sung, but the *gloria* was familiar. The tradition has remained, and *gloria in excelsis* is a frequent refrain in carols, such as 'Angels from the Realms of Glory', 'Ding Dong Merrily on High' and the Basque carol 'The Angel Gabriel'. Nowadays there is still a need to sing every carol in two languages: not Latin and English, but the languages of faith and of fun. When we sing 'While Shepherds Watched Their Flocks by Night' or 'Hark the Herald Angels Sing', we may or may not be affirming the message of the lyrics. Take 'While Shepherds Watched'. Arguably the first English hymn ever written, it originally appeared in the supplement to *A New Version of the Psalms of David* in 1700. In some editions it was entitled 'Song of the Angels at the Nativity of our Blessed Saviour'. Based on the angels' song from Luke 2:14, it is not a psalm, which is why it appeared in the supplement, allowed in as a scriptural paraphrase. The point is, a hymn such as this, which expounds and reflects upon the story of Christmas, is sung in pubs and schools by all and sundry, only some of whom are aware of, or believe in, what they are singing. Likewise with 'Hark the Herald Angels Sing': atheists and those of other faiths join in singing of the one who was 'born that man no more may die, born to raise the sons of earth, born to give them second birth'. Similarly, Christina Rossetti's 'In the Bleak Midwinter', set to music so beautifully by Gustav Holst, Harold Darke and more recently Bob Chilcott, concludes with the profound verse:

What can I give him,
poor as I am?
If I were a shepherd,
I would bring a lamb.
If I were a wise man,
I would do my part.
Yet what I can I give him,
give my heart.

One might reflect on what is going on internally for those who sing this carol but who do not mean anything by it. Others love singing carols, and they mean what they sing; such carol singing is macaronic in a modern sense: festive and faithful. Obviously, and delightfully, it is possible and desirable to be both. In doing so, and in being both, our hope and prayer is everyone might come to believe what they sing and sing what they believe. There are trivial carols and modern Christmas songs, some sillier than others. Yet even some of the Christmas classics have something to say to us, even if they make no mention of the nativity or incarnation. 'White Christmas' is a wonderful song, and there is no harm singing it (even if it is set in summertime). Songs about Santa are fun and flippant and stand in the Dickensian tradition of being kind, being with family and having fun. Many Christmas 'weepy' movies play this card too. Greg Lake, who wrote 'I Believe in Father Christmas' in 1974, has been accused of writing an anti-Christian song, yet it seems he wrote it as a protest against the commercialisation of Christmas and an affirmation of family warmth and forgiveness. What seems antithetical to the season might not be. Contrast this with 'It Came Upon the Midnight Clear', which was written by Edmund Sears, a unitarian who did not believe in the Christian Trinity. The carol does not mention Jesus at all, yet it is often sung at midnight services because it has the word 'midnight' in its first line and mentions Christmas themes, such as angels and peace on earth. 'Away in a Manger' is a hugely popular cradle carol, but its lyrics do not bear serious theological scrutiny.

Christmas carols can be complex. Yet carol singing is a wonderful, fun, unifying, reflective thing to do at this time of year. Long may it continue, and long may the angels' song and the story of salvation through incarnation resound in our churches, pubs, streets and concert halls.

Reflection

Do you think about what you sing? As you sing carols, reflect on what they are really saying to you and others.

Next time you sing or hear a carol, pay attention to the lyrics: are they true? Pray for all church musicians at this time of year, and give thanks for the gift of music.

Prayer (based on the Choristers' Prayer)

O Lord, grant that what we sing with our lips, we may believe in our hearts, and what we believe in our hearts, we may show forth in our lives. Amen

To order a copy of this book, please use the order form on page 149 or visit brfonline.org.uk.

Get to grips with the Bible

with these exceptionally useful short guides!

Each Really Useful Guide focuses on a specific biblical book, making it come to life for the reader, enabling them to understand the message and to apply its truth to today's circumstances. Though not a commentary, it gives valuable insight into the book's message. Though not an introduction, it summarises the important aspects of the book to aid reading and application.

Old Testament
Genesis 1—11
Genesis 12—50
Psalms
Edited by Simon P. Stocks
£5.99 or £6.99

brfonline.org.uk

New Testament
John
Romans
Colossians and Philemon
Edited by Derek Tidball
£5.99

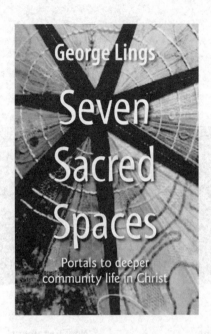

George Lings identifies seven characteristic elements in Christian communities through the ages, which when held in balance enable a richer expression of discipleship, mission and community. Through this model he explores how these elements relate to our individual and communal walk with God, hold good for family life and appear in wider society.

Seven Sacred Spaces
Portals to deeper community life in Christ
George Lings
978 0 85746 934 2 £12.99
brfonline.org.uk

To order

Online: **brfonline.org.uk**
Telephone: +44 (0)1865 319700
Mon–Fri 9.15–17.30

Delivery times within the UK are normally 15 working days. Prices are correct at the time of going to press but may change without prior notice.

Title	Price	Qty	Total
The Bible Doesn't Tell Me So	£8.99		
At Home in Advent	£8.99		
Really Useful Guides: Psalms	£6.99		
Really Useful Guides: Genesis 1—11, Genesis 12—50, John, Romans, Colossians and Philemon (*delete as appropriate)	£5.99 each		
Seven Sacred Spaces	£12.99		

POSTAGE AND PACKING CHARGES			
Order value	UK	Europe	Rest of world
Under £7.00	£2.00	Available on request	Available on request
£7.00–£29.99	£3.00		
£30.00 and over	FREE		

Total value of books	
Postage and packing	
Total for this order	

Please complete in BLOCK CAPITALS

Title _____ First name/initials _____ Surname_____

Address_____

_____ Postcode _____

Acc. No. _____ Telephone _____

Email_____

Method of payment

❑ Cheque (made payable to BRF) ❑ MasterCard / Visa

Card no. ☐☐☐☐ ☐☐☐☐ ☐☐☐☐ ☐☐☐☐

Expires end ☐☐ ☐☐ Security code* ☐☐☐ Last 3 digits on the reverse of the card

Signature* _____ Date _____ /_____ /_____
*ESSENTIAL IN ORDER TO PROCESS YOUR ORDER

Please return this form to:
BRF, 15 The Chambers, Vineyard, Abingdon OX14 3FE | **enquiries@brf.org.uk**
To read our terms and find out about cancelling your order, please visit **brfonline.org.uk/terms**.

The Bible Reading Fellowship (BRF) is a Registered Charity (233280)

BRF needs you!

If you're one of our regular *Guidelines* readers, you will know all about the rich rewards of regular Bible study and the value of serious daily notes to guide, inform and challenge you.

Here are some recent comments from *Guidelines* readers:

'… very thoughtful and spiritually helpful. [These notes] are speaking to the church as it is today, and therefore to Christians like us who live in today's world.'

'You have assembled an amazingly diverse group of people and their contributions are most certainly thoughtful.'

If you have similarly positive things to say about *Guidelines*, would you be willing to help spread the word about these valuable resources? One suggestion is to form a *Guidelines* reading group, not to take the place of private Bible study and prayer, but to give group members a chance to discover new dimensions and different interpretations as well as make new friends. It could be a breakfast or lunchtime meeting: short and to the point, or a more relaxed encounter, over a meal or a drink.

It doesn't need to be complicated: all *Guidelines* study notes have questions for reflection and suggestions for additional reading that lend themselves to group exploration.

We can supply further information if you need it and would love to hear about it if you do start a *Guidelines* reading group.

For more information:

- Email **enquiries@brf.org.uk**
- Telephone BRF on +44 (0)1865 319700 Mon–Fri 9.15–17.30
- Write to us at BRF, 15 The Chambers, Vineyard, Abingdon OX14 3FE

![BRF] Enabling all ages to grow in faith

At BRF, we long for people of all ages to grow in faith and understanding of the Bible. That's what all our work as a charity is about.

- Our **Living Faith** range of resources helps Christians go deeper in their understanding of scripture, in prayer and in their walk with God. Our conferences and events bring people together to share this journey.

- We also want to make it easier for local churches to engage effectively in ministry and mission – by helping them bring new families into a growing relationship with God through **Messy Church** or by supporting churches as they nurture the spiritual life of older people through **Anna Chaplaincy**.

- Our **Holy Habits** resources help whole congregations grow together as disciples of Jesus, living out and sharing their faith.

- Our **Parenting for Faith** team coaches parents and others to raise God-connected children and teens, and enables churches to fully support them.

- We also offer a professional education service, **Barnabas in Schools**, giving primary schools confidence, expertise and opportunities for exploring Christianity in creative ways that engage all pupils.

Do you share our vision?

Though a significant proportion of BRF's funding is generated through our charitable activities, we are dependent on the generous support of individuals, churches and charitable trusts.

If you share our vision, would you help us to enable even more people of all ages to grow in faith? Your prayers and financial support are vital for the work that we do. You could:

- Support BRF's ministry with a regular donation;
- Support us with a one-off gift;
- Consider leaving a gift to BRF in your will (see page 152);
- Encourage your church to support BRF as part of your church's giving to home mission – perhaps focusing on a specific ministry or programme;
- Most important of all, support BRF with your prayers.

Donate at **brf.org.uk/donate** or use the form on pages 153–54.

Building a legacy –
each person plays their part

Eliashib the high priest and his fellow priests went to work and rebuilt the Sheep Gate. They dedicated it and set its doors in place, building as far as the Tower of the Hundred, which they dedicated, and as far as the Tower of Hananel. The men of Jericho built the adjoining section, and Zakkur son of Imri built next to them.

NEHEMIAH 3:1–2 (NIV)

The 32 verses of Nehemiah 3 recount the story of the rebuilding of the walls of Jerusalem. A whole host of names follow in quick succession – perhaps not the Bible passage I would like to be asked to read aloud at the front of church for fear of mispronunciation.

Yet this chapter is one of my firm favourites from the whole of the Bible and one that I return to frequently.

The Bible affirms that each person is important, made in the image of God, and each person in the church has a part to play. The different parts come together to make the whole, and they cannot function without each other.

I know of many who at times have felt overstretched or underappreciated in their work and ministry – perhaps feeling that no one notices. Nehemiah 3 reminds us that every stone laid, every timber cut and every work undertaken is seen by God, and he knows his workers by name.

Throughout BRF's story, our ministry has grown beyond our expectation, thanks to those who have given generously, prayed faithfully and served tirelessly without seeking recognition.

They – and you – are known by God. Thank you. Could you help support this work?

Give – Pray – Get involved

If you would like some information about leaving a gift in your will to BRF, please get in touch with us on **+44 (0)1235 462305** or via **giving@brf.org.uk**.

brf.org.uk/lastingdifference

SHARING OUR VISION – MAKING A GIFT

I would like to make a gift to support BRF. Please use my gift for:

☐ Where it is most needed ☐ Anna Chaplaincy ☐ Barnabas in Schools
☐ Messy Church ☐ Parenting for Faith

Title	First name/initials	Surname

Address

	Postcode

Email

Telephone

Signature	Date

giftaid it You can add an extra 25p to every £1 you give.

Please treat as Gift Aid donations all qualifying gifts of money made

☐ today, ☐ in the past four years, ☐ and in the future.

I am a UK taxpayer and understand that if I pay less Income Tax and/or Capital Gains Tax in the current tax year than the amount of Gift Aid claimed on all my donations, it is my responsibility to pay any difference.

☐ My donation does not qualify for Gift Aid.

Please notify BRF if you want to cancel this Gift Aid declaration, change your name or home address, or no longer pay sufficient tax on your income and/or capital gains.

We will use your personal data to process this transaction. From time to time we may send information about the work of BRF that we think may be of interest to you. Our privacy policy is at **brf.org.uk/privacy**. Please contact us if you wish to discuss your mailing preferences.

Please complete other side of form ➲

SHARING OUR VISION – MAKING A GIFT

Regular giving

By Direct Debit: You can set up a Direct Debit quickly and easily at **brf.org.uk/donate**

By Standing Order: Please contact our Fundraising Administrator +44 (0)1865 319700 | **giving@brf.org.uk**

One-off donation

Please accept my gift of:

☐ £10 ☐ £50 ☐ £100   Other £ [＿＿＿＿＿]

by (*delete as appropriate*):

☐ Cheque/Charity Voucher payable to 'BRF'

☐ MasterCard/Visa/Debit card/Charity card

Name on card

Card no. [ ][ ][ ][ ] [ ][ ][ ][ ] [ ][ ][ ][ ] [ ][ ][ ][ ]

Expires end [M][M] [Y][Y]   Security code* [ ][ ][ ]

*Last 3 digits on the reverse of the card
ESSENTIAL IN ORDER TO PROCESS
YOUR PAYMENT

Signature   Date

☐ I would like to leave a gift to BRF in my will. Please send me further information.

Registered with

FR

FUNDRAISING
REGULATOR

For help or advice regarding making a gift, please contact our Fundraising Administrator +44 (0)1865 319700

⤺ Please complete other side of form

Please return this form to:
BRF, 15 The Chambers, Vineyard, Abingdon OX14 3FE

BRF

The Bible Reading Fellowship is a Registered Charity (233280)

GL0320

GUIDELINES SUBSCRIPTION RATES

Please note our new subscription rates, current until 30 April 2021:

Individual subscriptions
covering 3 issues for under 5 copies, payable in advance
(including postage & packing):

	UK	Europe	Rest of world
Guidelines 1-year subscription	£17.85	£25.80	£29.70
Guidelines 3-year subscription (9 issues)	£50.85	N/A	N/A

Group subscriptions
covering 3 issues for 5 copies or more, sent to one UK address (post free):

Guidelines 1-year subscription	£14.10 per set of 3 issues p.a.

Overseas group subscription rates
Available on request. Please email **enquiries@brf.org.uk**.

Copies may also be obtained from Christian bookshops:

Guidelines	£4.70 per copy

All our Bible reading notes can be ordered
online by visiting **brfonline.org.uk/collections/
subscriptions**

Guidelines is also available as
an app for Android, iPhone and iPad
brfonline.org.uk/collections/apps

GUIDELINES INDIVIDUAL SUBSCRIPTION FORM

All our Bible reading notes can be ordered online by visiting
brfonline.org.uk/collections/subscriptions

☐ I would like to take out a subscription:

Title _____ First name/initials _____ Surname _____

Address _____

_____ Postcode _____

Telephone _____ Email _____

Please send *Guidelines* beginning with the January 2021 / May 2021 /
September 2021 issue (*delete as appropriate*):

(*please tick box*)	UK	Europe	Rest of world
Guidelines 1-year subscription	☐ £17.85	☐ £25.80	☐ £29.70
Guidelines 3-year subscription	☐ £50.85	N/A	N/A

Total enclosed £ _____ (cheques should be made payable to 'BRF')

Please charge my MasterCard / Visa ☐ Debit card ☐ with £ _____

Card no. ☐☐☐☐ ☐☐☐☐ ☐☐☐☐ ☐☐☐☐

Expires end ☐☐☐☐ Security code* ☐☐☐ Last 3 digits on the reverse of the card

Signature* _____ Date _____/_____/_____
*ESSENTIAL IN ORDER TO PROCESS YOUR PAYMENT

To set up a Direct Debit, please also complete the Direct Debit instruction
on page 159 and return it to BRF with this form.

Please return this form to:
BRF, 15 The Chambers, Vineyard, Abingdon OX14 3FE

To read our terms and find out about cancelling your order, please visit **brfonline.org.uk/terms**.

The Bible Reading Fellowship (BRF) is a Registered Charity (233280)

GL0320

GUIDELINES GIFT SUBSCRIPTION FORM

☐ I would like to give a gift subscription (please provide both names and addresses):

Title .... First name/initials .... Surname ....

Address ....

.... Postcode ....

Telephone .... Email ....

Gift subscription name ....

Gift subscription address ....

.... Postcode ....

Gift message (20 words max. or include your own gift card):

....

....

Please send *Guidelines* beginning with the January 2021 / May 2021 / September 2021 issue (*delete as appropriate*):

(*please tick box*)	UK	Europe	Rest of world
Guidelines 1-year subscription	☐ £17.85	☐ £25.80	☐ £29.70
Guidelines 3-year subscription	☐ £50.85	N/A	N/A

Total enclosed £ .... (cheques should be made payable to 'BRF')

Please charge my MasterCard / Visa ☐ Debit card ☐ with £ ....

Card no. ☐☐☐☐ ☐☐☐☐ ☐☐☐☐ ☐☐☐☐

Expires end ☐☐ ☐☐   Security code* ☐☐☐   Last 3 digits on the reverse of the card

Signature* .... Date ...... /...... /......

*ESSENTIAL IN ORDER TO PROCESS YOUR PAYMENT

To set up a Direct Debit, please also complete the Direct Debit instruction on page 159 and return it to BRF with this form.

Please return this form to:
BRF, 15 The Chambers, Vineyard, Abingdon OX14 3FE

To read our terms and find out about cancelling your order, please visit **brfonline.org.uk/terms**.

The Bible Reading Fellowship (BRF) is a Registered Charity (233280)

DIRECT DEBIT PAYMENT

You can pay for your annual subscription to our Bible reading notes using Direct Debit. You need only give your bank details once, and the payment is made automatically every year until you cancel it. If you would like to pay by Direct Debit, please use the form opposite, entering your BRF account number under 'Reference number'.

You are fully covered by the Direct Debit Guarantee:

The Direct Debit Guarantee

- This Guarantee is offered by all banks and building societies that accept instructions to pay Direct Debits.
- If there are any changes to the amount, date or frequency of your Direct Debit, The Bible Reading Fellowship will notify you 10 working days in advance of your account being debited or as otherwise agreed. If you request The Bible Reading Fellowship to collect a payment, confirmation of the amount and date will be given to you at the time of the request.
- If an error is made in the payment of your Direct Debit, by The Bible Reading Fellowship or your bank or building society, you are entitled to a full and immediate refund of the amount paid from your bank or building society.
- If you receive a refund you are not entitled to, you must pay it back when The Bible Reading Fellowship asks you to.
- You can cancel a Direct Debit at any time by simply contacting your bank or building society. Written confirmation may be required. Please also notify us.

The Bible Reading Fellowship

Instruction to your bank or building society to pay by Direct Debit

Please fill in the whole form using a ballpoint pen and return it to:
BRF, 15 The Chambers, Vineyard, Abingdon OX14 3FE

Service User Number: | 5 | 5 | 8 | 2 | 2 | 9 |

Name and full postal address of your bank or building society

To: The Manager	Bank/Building Society
Address	
	Postcode

Name(s) of account holder(s)

Branch sort code

Bank/Building Society account number

Reference number

Instruction to your Bank/Building Society
Please pay The Bible Reading Fellowship Direct Debits from the account detailed in this instruction, subject to the safeguards assured by the Direct Debit Guarantee. I understand that this instruction may remain with The Bible Reading Fellowship and, if so, details will be passed electronically to my bank/building society.

Signature(s)

Banks and Building Societies may not accept Direct Debit instructions for some types of account.